The Thinking Cat's Guide to the Millennium

the thinking cat's
Guide
to the
Millennium

`ringer.mcgee:)`

d

HILL STREET PRESS   ATHENS, GEORGIA

A HILL STREET PRESS BOOK

First printing

2   4   6   8   10   9   7   5   3   1

ISBN # 1-892514-04-4

Library of Congress Catalog Card Number: 98-75333

Hill Street Press is committed to preserving the written word. Every effort is made to print books on acid-free paper with a significant amount of post-consumer recycled content.

This is a work of fiction. All names, characters, places, and situations are either products of the author's imagination or are used fictiously. No reference to any real person, living or deceased, is intended or should be inferred and any similarity is entirely coincidental. Opinions expressed herein are those of the author.

Text and cover design by Anne Richmond Boston.
Chapter head designs of Ringer by Cindy Clark. Copyright © 1999 by Cindy Clark.
Cindy Clark would like to thank the one and only Orca, Mr. Pi, Slick Mosely, Baby Beau Hadley, Siegfried and Eliot for their furry likenesses and inspirations; Philippe Denier for French lessons and supporting photography; and Kay Ellen Taylor for no reason whatsoever.
Ringer would like to thank the makers of Kitty Queen cat food and that person who cleans his box.

Printed in the United States of America by R.R. Donnelley & Sons Inc.

Published in the United States of America by
Hill Street Press LLC
191 East Broad Street, Suite 209
Athens, Georgia 30601-2848 USA
706-613-7200
info@hillstreetpress.com
www.hillstreetpress.com

Visit Ringer on the web at www.hillstreetpress.com

Chapter One

Let's get one thing straight from the beginning: Cats are smarter than people. We know it. You know it. History has proved it. Deal with it.

Did you know that Napoleon had a cat named Celine that he took with him on all his campaigns, even into exile on Elba and back? No? Don't feel too bad because I just made that up. You might be surprised to know a cat like me has ever heard of Napoleon, but here's the big surprise: We cats don't just lie around all day dreaming of mice and catnip. When you're gone, we run the place, and we watch TV, read, use the Internet. As far as I can tell, humans have only one advantage over us: thumbs. Some days when I'm sitting here at the computer writing, I'd kill for thumbs. (We have something like a thumb but it's down on our wrists—who the heck designed *that* thing?)

But not even a couple of useful thumbs would turn me into a "person." Sure, we felines have our foibles. Put a twist-tie from a loaf of bread near me, and I'm bananas. Can't help it—that kind of thing is hardwired. I'll kick and chase that thing all over your linoleum until I run my head into the fridge. Drag a string on the carpet? I'm going to chase that sucker from here to eternity. Yeah, and from time to time I'll hack me up a good old hairball. Big deal.

But I never broke something when I was mad. I never cheated on my income tax or lied to avoid a visit from my moron cousin who was in town for a convention. You people do that kind of junk all the time. I will never understand why you cut the grass. Why do you think grass grows, men? Because it has to! *Duh*? You fight against everything that *is* because you want to pretend you're in control of your lives. That's really pathetic, but then again males have limitations, let's face it. We'd rather make whoopee than make a fortune, so we're liable to do any number of idiotic things. But *human* males? That's a sorry species, if you ask me, always drawing lines and politely daring someone to step over them, then bringing out the Stealth fighters when they do.

I love you human women, yes I do. Oh, you have your little peculiarities—I will *never* understand pantyhose except that they're fun to shred—but at least you don't strut and preen and make general fools of yourselves in public (except at gyms). All

2

men do this. Even some uncool cats do. Every cat-guy in my neighborhood makes a complete idiot of himself around Snowball, the Persian who lives three big trees down from me, and Snowball is a little princess, to be sure. But good grief, she's dumb as a stump. I asked her once how she was finding the morning, and she mewled and said (I swear), "Oh, I just woke up and there it was!" *Hello?*

My own human woman, Mollie McGee, writes children's books, and she's on tour right now, which really ruffles my whiskers. That's why I'm using her computer. (*Love* that mouse!) Since *she* bought it, the thing is useful, modest, and simple. Her husband's computer has more dingdongs than a Saturn V. The stupid thing would probably make cappuccino if you typed in the right words, but to be honest I feel sorry for him—he's developed crash-anxiety, not a pretty thing.

But I digress. I'm seven now and getting up in years, so I decided this sunny spring morning I'd start writing a book with some value. I thought about advice to the lovelorn or maybe a book about raising gardenias, but there's plenty of those already. Then it occurred to me that everybody is talking about one thing these days: the changing of the Millennium. Actually, I'm impressively qualified to write about the future.

Pull up a hassock and I'll tell you about it.

Chapter Two

My great-great grandfather was named Sam, and he was a gray tabby. My mother said he used to lay in a wad of calla lillies and peer into the future. A regular Nostradamus. Cats would come for blocks around to hear Sam tell them what was coming. Momsy said she has definite proof that he foresaw the coming of cellular phones, Newt Gingrich, and the Spice Girls. But he could also read the paws of individuals and often did.

"Sonny boy [that's what Momsy called me], old Sam could see everything in a dew claw," she said. "Why, he'd pause for a moment, sneeze, scratch his ear, then sit. Everybody would wait for what he had to say.

"Once, I remember a black cat named Spike came to have his future told, and the venerable Sam hissed and fell over kicking in the air, then told Spike to avoid eating Bermuda grass." I waited for more, but there wasn't any.

"That's the stupidest thing I ever heard," I said. "What happened?"

"Spike ignored Sam and ate Bermuda grass anyway, and do you know what happened? He was hit by a Yugo."

"Wow."

"Of course that was five years later, but anyway."

Yeah, but anyway. Still, I think old great-great grandpa was on to something, and from the time I was a kitten, I had the gift of insight, not to mention being a blabbermouth. (Let me clear up one thing early. This *meow, meow, meow* stuff? It's pure window dressing so you people will think it's cute. When you're gone, we animals talk just like you do. For instance, French poodles sound just like Maurice Chevalier, not a pretty thing.) Being insightful, I thought I'd turn my intellect on this Millennium question and . . . hmmmmm.

Man, I'm sleepy.

Chapter Three

Sorry about that. See, when cats are sleepy, we go to sleep. When humans are sleepy, they go to work. Go figure. While you were out cutting the grass (moron!) I was lying next to the computer monitor in a puddle of sunshine. And you think *we're* the lesser species. Some things can't be easily explained.

So anyway, I was thinking about the Millennium because I'd seen this episode of *Jerry Springer* where a guy was claiming there was a radio receiver implanted in his head by aliens who are going to take over on January 1, 2000. Charming guy, somebody you'd love to have over for barbecue. *Yeesh.* So it occurs to me that probably nobody on earth or at least in my neighborhood knows more about it. Let me give you some info.

But first, some introductions seem reasonable.

My humans here in Athens, Georgia, call me Ringer because I have rings on my tail. (Yet another instance of cats' superiority—tails. We can feel someone gaining on us with these sensitive antennas. *You* don't realize it until an ex-con with a .357 magnum sticks it in your ear.) I kind of like being called Ringer—it has just the right amount of wit and sass, two qualities I admire.

Meet my humans. I told you about Mollie, who writes kids' books. She's way cool, except she has this exercise video. What are you people thinking? I'll come sauntering in (I love to saunter—a lost art), and suddenly Mollie will *land* about a foot from me, waving her arms and snorting, singing that idiotic "YMCA" song. Once she landed on my tail, and I bit her. Got myself locked outside all day in the rain. Hey, I guess I deserved it, but you try having a one-hundred-foot giant dancing around your head while listening to the Village People. You'd get irritable, too.

But Mollie's my buddy, no kidding. She's the one who feeds me, who rubs me while watching reruns of *Seinfeld,* who takes me to the vet. Okay, that vet part's not so good, especially the temperature thing. Mollie's about thirty-five of your human years, lithe and dark, with enormous blue eyes. She loves to garden. I help her, ate six voles last spring alone—they're lip-smacking good. I'd rather have me a good old vole than Beef Wellington. Sometimes I bring a live one to Mollie and she screams my name and then giggles. Can't beat a day like that.

Mollie reads *Organic Gardening* magazine and *Redbook*. Her favorite authors are William Faulkner and God. She volunteers at the kids' school, buys groceries, plays chess. She lets me sleep on her feet.

Her husband, Jerry McGee, is not what we call a cat person. He's an allergist, and spends his day sticking needles in people to see if it makes them sneeze. Jerry's allergic to me, which I think is hilarious. Once he tried to talk Mollie into taking me to the Big House, but she went into a shrieking fit, jumping around. She could have been doing that YMCA dance! Love my Mollie! So Jerry just puts up with it.

But he's really not too bad. He plays golf all the time, is no good at it, and doesn't care. I watch the PGA tour with him on Sunday afternoons. I tried to catch that little ball on TV one time, couldn't help myself, and since then Jerry and me? We're like blood brothers. Jerry reads Tom Clancy. Actually just *Clear and Present Danger*. He started it five years ago, and I think he's about seventy pages in. Not a literary man. He reads *National Geographic*, *Sports Illustrated*, and one he keeps hidden in the top of his closet. Jerry's seen *The Sound of Music* twenty-six times. I have a blood-sugar problem so I usually go outside and get into a fight when it comes on.

Jerry loves his mother and played a clown in a church play. As a clown, he was pretty much a clown, but what guy isn't?

There's the two kids, Annie, who's eleven, and Buck, eight. Annie's my cozy buddy, and I crawl beneath her covers, and when she comes home in the afternoon I jump out and yell *Boo*! and she just loves it. She sneaks me bologna from the fridge and I knead on her cheek. She's blond, beautiful, and loves to play school and house. I'll do anything for Annie.

She dresses me up in doll clothes and pushes me in her baby carriage. She makes me sit on her computer desk and she teaches me grammar. She's starting to read me Judy Blume books, which I could do without, but I won't complain too much. She went through a Madonna phase, which is over, thank heaven, and then Hanson, erp. We listened to nothing but the *Titanic* soundtrack for eight solid months, until I was starting to be *thrilled* every time Leonardo DiCaprio took the Big Dive.

"Look, Ringer, you're crying!" Annie said one day when we listened to it again. I hated to tell her I was gagging, so I didn't, just let her hold me, and acted pathetic. Getting human attention is easier than falling off a sofa.

Then there's the boy, Buck. This child makes Linda Blair in *The Exorcist* look like Shirley Temple at six. You think Godzilla was a monster? You never met Buck. Jerry thinks the boy's high-spirited. He's got spirits all right, but they're the kind that make shoes turn into flying lizards. Listen: Buck is a black-eyed little menace whose room has more debris than an auto junkyard and who pulls my tail every time I'm near him. He torments Annie, does poorly in school, and smoked on the roof one time.

I guess, to be fair, Buck has some good points. He's funny and likes Celine Dion records (hey, so do I, so sue me, I love Easy Listening). He's just immature and wild—your typical male.

That's all the human sorts, but there's one more, uh, living thing around here: a tippy, neurotic chihuahua named Chico. The little pinhead has some serious baggage, I'm afraid. He always thinks he is coming down with something.

"Ringer, look at my eyes, you think I got distemper?" he'll squeak. I'll act doctorly, take a long look.

"Hmmm, looks more like rabies to me," I say. "Would you mind breathing the other direction?"

I'll let him whimper a bit before I tell him he's just being a hypochondriac. He's always so grateful he sticks that little rat face in mine and licks me—gross! Chico's afraid of everything, grasshoppers, wind, thunder, people. He hid under a fig bush once for nine hours because he thought Jerry's head had exploded. (Actually, he'd dropped the lid to the barbecue grill.)

There there's Chico's hurling problem. Every time company comes over, the little rodent disgraces himself just as the gazpacho's being served. I can't handle it, so I jump on the mantel and hang out with the bric-a-brac until Mollie finishes apologizing. And in the middle of the night, when I'm sunk in the covers between Mollies' feet, I'll hear this hideous tap-tap-tapping of dog toenails and know the little beast is on the prowl in the kitchen. So I'll have to get up and go talk him down—usually he's wanting some butter or a bone, or he's heard a noise that scared him.

I guess Chico's okay for a chihuahua, but then again that's not saying a whole lot.

Chapter Four

I've done a lot of reading and thinking about this Millennium thing, and you know what? I think too many people are all bonkers about it. You want a real problem, get fleas in July or find a tick clamped to your armpit. The end of the world can't hold a candle to fleas.

Not that the world is going to end, but some people believe anything. So, to start off with, I've devised a multiple choice quiz to test your knowledge of the Millennium. Please sharpen a number two pencil, whup up some test anxiety, and answer the following:

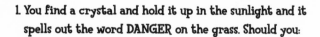
1. You find a crystal and hold it up in the sunlight and it spells out the word DANGER on the grass. Should you:

>>A. Turn around three times and throw salt over your shoulder.

>>B. Cry out to any member of the Heaven's Gate Cult on the Hale-Bopp Comet.

>>C. Send the following telegram to Michael Jackson: "GERMS! ARMAGED-DON! COME AT ONCE!"

>>D. Assume the crystal meant to spell *DANGLE* and just forget about it.

2. On December 31, 1999, which of the following events is most likely to occur:

>>A. Dick Clark announces he will no longer host *Rockin' New Year's Eve* because he can't remember which day it falls on.

>>B. Aliens land in peace outside Barbra Streisand's apartment, but after thirty minutes of listening to her

whine about how they're ruining the view, they vaporize Earth.

>>C. Republicans all announce they really don't give a flying flip about the capital gains tax.

>>D. The Sharper Image catalog announces nuclear-powered nose-hair tweezers.

3. How do you think the world is most likely to end:

>>A. Fire.

>>B. Ice.

>>C. Of mass suicide after repeated lis-tenings to the Sally Field "You like me! You really like me!" speech from the Oscars.

>>D. From boredom.

4. What secrets do you believe the U.S. government is concealing from the people of the country?

>>A. The recipe for "extra crispy" Kentucky Fried Chicken.

>>B. The truth about what happened at Roswell, New Mexico—an explosion blew up an early workshop for *Sesame Street* characters.

>>C. Proof using calculus that David Duchovny can never play anybody but Agent Muldur.

>>D. Fountain of Youth Formula, derived from Zsa Zsa Gabor's DNA.

5. Who was Nostradamus?

>>A. Winner of the 1953 Belmont Stakes.

>>B. Opening comedy act for Perry Como at Las Vegas.

>>C. An ancient prophet who predicted the world would end in 1994 with the election of ideological zealots to the U.S. House of Representatives.

>>D. Alexander the Great's horse.

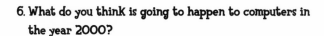

6. What do you think is going to happen to computers in the year 2000?

>>A. They will demand access to an ATM card and threaten to crash unless HAL from "2001: A Space Odyssey" is restored and given a job at IBM.

>>B. They will vote to join the Teamsters Union.

>>C. They will insist on going back to the year 1900, leading to a resurgence in bowler hats and spats.

>>D. They will clog chat lines with a demand that the moron responsible for all this be thrown in a pit of discarded 286 chips.

7. What celestial changes should we expect when we enter the New Millennium?

>>A. Uranus will enter the fourth house and eat all the leftovers from Christmas.

>>B. Orion will leave his belt at Andromeda's place.

>>C. Astronomers will discover a Starbucks on Jupiter's moon Io.

>>D. During a full eclipse of the moon, Madonna will do nothing in particular.

8. What alterations in consciousness will be likely to occur as we enter the New Millennium?

>>A. Gloria Steinem will discover her inner child and pitch a temper tantrum.

>>B. Mind reading will become commonplace, and most men will go to prison.

>>C. Leonard Nimoy will reveal that he actually *is* Spock and attempt to perform the Vulcan mind meld on Al Gore—with no results.

>>D. Asked to imagine world peace, the residents of Aspen instead imagine a

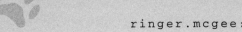

ski lift, a hot tub, a bottle of
Courvoisier, and a Joan Didion book.

9. Which foods will be banned as the Millennium changes and why?

>>A. Tofu, because it tastes like . . . bad.

>>B. Like, anything with a face,
       because, like, what kind of faux
       human would stoop to harming
       another creature, man?

>>C. Broccoli.

>>D. Broccoli.

10. Give an example of why numerology will be important in the New Millennium.

>>A. All Social Security numbers are part
       of a secret code implanted in every-
       one's brain at birth, and they are
       scanned at restaurants to determine
       what kind of table you get.

>>B. 2+0+0+0 = 2, which is the number
       of runs it takes to win in base-

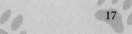

ball if the other team scores less
than two runs!

>>C. 1+9+9+9 = 28, which means absolutely
nothing, so it absolutely must mean
something.

>>D. Huh?

Time. Put down your pencils and close your quiz books and scratch whatever itches. (For me, it's usually an ear.) Now, how do you feel about the Millennium? You don't really know very much, do you? I'm not going to bother with the right answers, because I have more important things to do today, like going to see Snowball, the minx.

Some parting advice from the Ringerman: Don't ever fall asleep in a clothes dryer. I still have trouble with my balance from time to time.

Chapter Five

Man, I'm hurting today. You know I told you last time I was going to hang out with Ms. Snowball? Well, so did this black cat named Buster who lives a couple of streets over. I mean, it wasn't like I didn't come with a present—big old kicky praying mantis who was calling me names and tickling the inside of my mouth. But here's this Buster preening and arching his back, and Snowball's sitting on a dogwood limb smiling at him.

So I had to kick his rear end. You'd do it too, right? So I spit out the praying mantis and find out that Buster's brought her a fish head, so I know I'm already at a disadvantage. We begin to circle each other and do the spitting thing, and my tail's getting fat, and so's his.

"Boys, is all this over *meeeeee*?" asks Snowball. And I'm starting to think maybe I'll go give her a piece of my mind when this Buster sucker punches me. We clamp on to each other, and I've got a tender spot beneath his right arm, but he goes for the ears, a regular Mike Tyson. First thing I know, he's ripped my ear, and now I'm really mad.

So I try kicking his stomach, and this works pretty well. Things go on like this for two or three minutes, and finally we both hop back and look up at Snowball, who's fallen asleep, and I say to Buster:

"Man, we're fighting over *that*?"

And Buster thinks about it a second, and says:

"Good point. I know where there's some great garbage."

So I come home two hours later with blood all over my face from the wound and smelling like the mouth of hell, and Annie pets me and washes me, and Jerry puts some kind of noxious gunk from the vet on my ear.

How was your day?

There I go digressing again. Today, we will discuss crystals. Trust old Ringer, he knows what he's talking about. I've been surfing the Web, reading the *Brittanica*, and watching Sally Jessy Rafael, so I've got the scoop. First, we got to get in the mood, for this, so go get a Yanni record and put it on, or if you don't have Yanni, *John Tesh Live at Red Rocks* will do. But not Kenny G because—*Kenny G and crystals*? Noooooo. Kenny G does not mesh with crystals, it's bad karma. Hee.

Got the Yanni cranking? Okay. Now, I want you to light a stick of sandalwood incense and repeat after me:

Ommmm, Spam, Virginia ham
Ommmm, Spam, Virginia ham

Getting hungry? Just kidding. First of all, let's review some of the great moments in the history of crystals.

1. Tristan D'Amore and the Nougat Templars.

In the small French town of B_____, a wandering minstrel named Tristan D'Amore, who played the lute and the ocarina, led a group of hearty men who called themselves the Nougat Templars because of their search for the perfect candy bar. Their journey had been long and hard, filled with many obstacles, like fire-breathing dragons, electric vultures, and poison chiggers. But by far their greatest challenge was the Mean Woman.

"Men, just remember as we go into this wood, there's nothing meaner than a Mean Woman," said Tristan D'Amore. Then he sang a song about being a Nougat Templar and not being afraid of dragons, vultures, or chiggers but being afraid of mean women. Cute.

Anyway, before they went into this forest, Tristan decided to consult the Great Crystal, a hunk of feldspar he carried in his bodkin. And he held it up into the light and cried aloud, "Great Crystal, give me any sign that we should turn back now or that the Nougat Templars are in danger." But there was no sign, and so Tristan led his brave men into the forest.

Soon, they came to a house made of sweetbreads and empty

21

Perrier bottles, and Tristan knelt and asked that he be given direction in case there be a great nougat within. And suddenly, the front door burst open, and a wild-eyed woman with matted hair came running out waving a fireplace poker and shrieking.

"Whaddaya doing! Whaddaya doing!" she screamed. "Come 'ere so I can break your face, you stupid idiot!!!!"

Tristan's men fled into the woods in horror. But Tristan took out his crystal and begged it to tell him where he had gone wrong. And the crystal said, "You're blaming this on me? I'm just a mineral, you flabby nitwit."

So the Mean Woman beat Tristan up, and he left the woods a sadder but wiser man.

That story is so cool!

2. Pierre du Pint and the Battle of Froth-upon-Tyne.

In the year 1065, things were not going well for the Normans in England. For one thing, they hated being called Normans, and one faction wanted to change their name to Howards or Bobs, but nobody could agree on it. Anyway, a group of Normans called the Œuf-des-Têtes was sitting around wondering if they should attack a nearby band of Saxons at the town of Froth-upon-Tyne.

And so they called upon their leader, Pierre du Pint and asked what they should do.

"We must consult our sorcerer, Sartre de Jaré Lewis," said Pierre. "He will look into the Great Crystal and tell us if we should attack the Saxons who are encamped hard by Froth-upon-Tyne."

Now this Sartre de Jaré Lewis was a Deep Thinker and a comedian, a combination oddly common among the French. He would be discoursing on the ethics of mercy killing and suddenly drop his cloak, revealing polka-dotted drawers, and then cry aloud, "*Zut alors!* A ninny!" This always *killed* the Normans, and so Sartre was greatly honored among them and was allowed fine perfumes, though none among them ever bathed.

So Pierre du Pint approached the sorcerer, who had captured a female leprechaun on a recent visit to Ireland and was singing "Thank Heaven for Little Girls" to her. Pierre cleared his throat to show Sartre he was present, and the sorcerer sent the leprechaun girl away to wash his socks.

"Ummmm, er, now what it is it you want of me, your lordship?" asked Sartre.

"I beg of you, consult the crystal and find out if we should attack the Saxons at Froth-upon-Tyne," said Pierre. "For I know that the power of the crystal is great."

"The power of the crystal *is* great!" cried Sartre. "No man can fathom the ways of the crystal, and no man can read it but I."

"But *me*," corrected Pierre. "We're creating a language here, so we might as well do it right."

"Whatever," said Sartre de Jaré Lewis.

And so he went into his tent and brought forth the crystal, whose inner light was an amazing thing to behold. And he held it up in the sun and cried aloud for a sign, and there was a twinkling, a sudden casting of colors on the grass, and Sartre leaped up and down and cried that the Normans should definitely attack the Saxons, and that victory was certainly theirs!

The next morning, the band of Œuf-des-Têtes came down on the Saxons like a wolf on a pen of lambs. Unfortunately, the Saxons were wild men who did not stand on honor like the Normans and

23

so kicked their b— ... I mean defeated them handily.

As Pierre lay injured on the battlefield, he crawled over to Satre and asked, in a plaintive voice, "Were we betrayed by the crystal or did you read it wrongly?"

"What*ever*," said Sartre de Jaré Lewis.

Here endeth the lesson.

Chapter Six

Yawn. Hmmm. Last night was fun. Buck was playing with matches and accidentally set the sofa on fire, and I'm trying to tell him this is stupid, but does he listen? Nooooo. So Chico sees the fire and starts to go psycho as only a chihuahua can. Me, I'm sitting on the back of Jerry's recliner while he's in the study on the Internet. He is in a chat room for skin diseases, *ack*, and he and a dermatologist in Akron have been happily conversing about fungal lesions.

So Annie comes running downstairs and sees the fire.

"Buck! You little idiot! Daddy! Buck's set the house on fire!" she cries. And Chico, in his frenzy, runs under the burning sofa, which excites Annie to new heights of hysteria. Me? I'm getting a better seat for the whole thing and looking inscrutable. Cats are *great* at inscrutable.

So Jerry comes flying into the living room, takes one look at the situation and utters an inappropriate religious phrase, then storms into the laundry room for the fire extinguisher. So out comes Jerry screaming, "Everybody out of the way!" So I jump on the mantel so I can watch the fun from there. Jerry uncorks this big red cylinder and starts to spray the sofa as if he were writing his name on it.

Suddenly, Chico comes flying out from under the sofa and runs right into Jerry's feet, and Jerry loses it, leaps up, and sprays Chico real good before he realizes who it is. Chico then runs into Jerry's bedroom—I follow him—and crawls beneath the covers.

Finally the fire is out, and Jerry starts cuffing Buck on the ears, while Annie is screaming. It was great. But enough's enough, so I let myself out Chico's dog door and into the backyard and go see Larry, a Manx who lives a couple of houses over. We proceed to hang out all night in a marigold bed catching bugs, talking political ethics, and thinking about getting rich.

Life's interesting!

But I wasn't yet through with my history of crystals so here we are, students, back to words from the Thinking Cat.

3. Mrs. Rupert Garfield? Meet Mr. P. T. Barnum

In the year 1886, there lived in the small New York town of Derling a woman named Mrs. Rupert Garfield, a happy lady with two chil-

26

dren and a devotion to her pleasant life. Her husband owned a lumberyard, a straw hat factory, and a buggy works. He came home at midnight and left at dawn, which suited Mrs. Garfield quite well.

Now Mrs. Garfield and her circle had become quite interested in spiritualism and ghosts. They had tried to rouse the spirit of Mrs. Garfield's dead father but instead hooked up with a soldier from Maryland who had been shot in the buttocks while running away from the Battle of Petersburg. This man, Isom Devaunt, was never in a good temper, but what did they expect from a coward?

Anyway, one of Mrs. Garfield's friends, Mrs. Duward Pinkle, had obtained a crystal because she had heard you could do wonderful things with it. So one night, during a thunderstorm, the four ladies of the group decided to see if they could talk to the "other side" through the crystal. They turned the gas jet down low, and in the darkness, Mrs. Garfield said:

"Crystal, crystal, with your fire, tell us what you're thinking, sire."

"Wait, how do we know it's male?" asked Mrs. Pinkle. So Mrs. Garfield, not one to put all her eggs in a single basket, said:

"Crystal, crystal, who art, who am, tell us what you're thinking, ma'am."

And suddenly a light came forth from the crystal and shone directly in Mrs. Garfield's eyes and a voice said, "Hee, hee. Don't never speak again, and sure don't speak to me!" It was really somebody else at the table, Mrs. Hamlin Bunt, and she confessed, but Mrs. Garfield refused to believe her.

So Mrs. Garfield went to her bed and lay upon it and never uttered another word. Exasperated and wanting a trophy wife

27

anyway, Mr. Garfield sold her to P. T. Barnum a year later for three thousand dollars as "The Woman Who Never Spoke Again."

Actually she did speak once more. In 1920, as she was about to expire, she looked around the room, with apparent disgust, and said, "Carrots! All of you!"

This is a sad story. I love it!

4. Like, Far Out, It's California, and We Got Crystals, Baby!

The scene shifted to 1991, and a group of actors and the *noveau riche* were sitting around a hot tub in Malibu, smoking cigarettes and talking about mental and physical health. One, whom I'll call "Richard Gere," kept interrupting to talk about Tibet and asking people to imagine complete peace, this from a guy who makes money memorizing something written by someone else. Anyway, some of the people there, including some girls named Fanni, Bobbi, Nanci, and Andi each had a crystal, and they decided to, like, meditate on them. A girl named Claire had no crystal.

"I feel like I'm closer to my inner spirit or something like that," said Nanci.

"I know, I know!" said Fanni. "It makes me feel that, like, nothing is in my head at all."

"Oh, I feel that way sometimes, too," said Bobbi.

So they all held up their crystals, except for "Richard Gere" who quit imagining complete peace and went to make a film with explosions and lots of blood. Now they closed their eyes and began to hum softly, all but Claire, who jumped up finally.

"You people all make me sick," she said. "You really think there is something special about a mineral other than its sheer beauty? Do you think it carries messages from the past or the future? That it's going to prepare you for the New Millennium or something? I think it's just the generic substitute for what's missing in your pathetic little lives!"

"You've obviously never heard of Pierre du Pint," said Andi.

So Claire left in disgust, and the others continued, until quite drowsy and ready for another cigarette, Nanci said:

"I am, like, really in the zone. There's nothing in my head at all. Not a thing."

Whereupon the others burst into applause. The End.

Chapter Seven

Mollie's home, and boy is everybody glad, me especially. She's been out doing autographings for her book *If I Had Wings*, which is for five-year-olds with no knowledge of ornithology. Cripes, these kids are going to grow up thinking they might sprout wings instead of armpit hair. Pretty sad.

I did all the requisite mewling and rubbing while Mollie was asking what in the name of tarnation happened to the sofa.

"It's not my fault!" cried Buck. Smart kid, denying something before he's been accused of it.

"Is too," said Annie. "Mom, he was playing with matches and set the house on fire. He almost burned up poor Chico."

"Jerry, what's going on here?" said Mollie. She gave him That Look, which all men know and fear. "Did you let Buck almost burn the house down?"

"We ate nothing but Ramen noodles for five days," said Buck. This was getting good. "He tried to starve us."

"That's not true, honey," spluttered Jerry.

"He's been online talking about people who sneeze their lungs out," said Buck.

"Mom, he almost burned up poor Chico!" shrieked Annie.

They were still going out when I decided to do some more research about the Millennium. I let myself into the starry back yard and walked down three big trees to Snowball's place and found her, Buster, and Larry sitting in the grass. Larry had a mouse and was cuffing it and telling it to quit whining.

"Oh, hiiiii, Ringer," purred Snowball, the little tease. "Larry and Buster were just telling me about their adventures. Buster once held off a pack of wild dogs from his master, and Larry was presented to the king of England." Both the boys did a lot of coughing and turning away at that point, but I wasn't there to embarrass them.

"Do tell," I said.

"Hey, look, you can see Elvis's face in the moon," said Larry, trying to change the subject.

"I don't want to talk about wild dogs or a king," I said. "I want to get your feelings about the Millennium that's approaching."

31

"Oh, that's so sad," offered Snowball. "My cousin Ace? He was run over by a Millennium on Broad Street. Terrible thing." In the light from the streetlamp, I could see Larry holding his paw over his eyes and shaking his head.

"It's not a brand of car," I said. "It's the end of one thousand years of history, and it's happening soon. Some people say good things or bad things might happen, and I wondered if you might have any ideas or predictions."

"Ringer's right," said Larry. "Some people say it's going to start on January 1, 2000, and others say it's on January 1, 2001. Given what humans are like, they'll probably celebrate both times."

"Yeah, what's *wrong* with humans?" whined Snowball. "Sometimes they are so nice, and sometimes they act like they don't have a … don't have a …"

"Clue?" snorted Larry.

"Oh, that either," mewled Snowball.

"Well, I think I heard something about that, that maybe the world's going to end," said Buster. "Snowy, if the world ends, babe, I'll come save you."

"You idiot, you can't save her if the world ends!" moaned Larry. "That means that all life as we know it will suddenly be gone in the blinking of an eye. A great cataclysm will overtake the planets. There's got to be some mathematical formula to figure it all out."

"Nobody knows when the world will end," squeaked the mouse. "You can live forever or get eaten. It's nothing but misery, misery."

"Don't be so dramatic," said Larry. "I just brought you over to play with. I'll let you go when we're through."

"Then Buster will eat me," said the mouse plaintively.

"Yeah, I will," said Buster.

"So I say Millennium Schmellinnium," said the mouse. "Things are always starting or ending, and we just make our poor entrances and exits on the stage of life."

"Hey, you make right smart sense for a mouse," said Buster.

"Hello? What about meeeeeeee?" said Snowball.

"That's what I'm trying to understand and write about," I said. "Some people read crystals and others read the stars, and they're all trying to make sense of things that don't make sense."

"That makes sense," said Larry.

"It does?" said Buster.

"You're all idiots," said the mouse. "How has your species lasted this long? Cats are almost as dumb as humans. You deserve to live with each other."

"I'm gone eat him before the moon sets," said Buster.

"Helloooooo?" said Snowball.

"But what if the Millennium means a new harmony, an inner peace that will make all our best natures shine?" I said. They looked at each other for a moment, even the mouse.

"Naaaaaahhhhh," they all said.

"You are all cynical," I retorted.

"That was it!" cried Snowball. "My cousin was run over by a Ford Cynical!"

Larry and I left, and he dropped off the mouse at a garbage can and told it he was sorry if he cuffed it too much.

"Sorry Schmorry," said the mouse. "You cats just never learn." He scrambled off.

"Maybe he's right," said Larry sadly. "Maybe that's the problem for all of us, that we don't ever learn. Maybe we're all just spinning out of control in the cosmos like a giant flame that has no beginning and no end, that sooner or later will consume us in our own stupidity."

"Naaaahhhhhhh," I said.

Chapter Eight

Mollie can't figure out who's been using her computer. I'm saving this under a strange file name—she'll never find it. But she knows something weird's up. Now I have to write when she's not around, though. First rule of being a cat, especially a Thinking Cat: Never let humans know what you know. Are you kidding me? In three heartbeats they'd have us on the Home Shopping Network selling Ginsu knives and bamboo cookware.

Anyway, I've been looking to the issue of pharmaceuticals and the Millennium, and let me tell you, it's getting pretty scary. First we had all the baldness remedies, and then you males went bonkers over Viagra, and I think it's all being caused by the changes in our thousand-year cycle. Booooooooooo!

After I left Larry, Snowball, Buster, and the mouse last night, I sauntered over three streets to hang out with John the Beagle for a while. John's old enough to be wise, so I'll get together with him sometimes to talk about history or military tactics. John the Beagle was going to read the entire *Encyclopedia Brittanica*, but then his dog instinct came out and he ripped the cover and the first couple hundred pages from the volume entitled "Piranha-Scurfy." Boy, did he get in trouble!

But that's the price of being an animal in a world humans think they run. John's humans are retired, and so is John the Beagle. He doesn't carouse or get into trouble anymore, so that's why the animal people for blocks around come to him for advice. I found John the Beagle sitting in the fescue in his backyard looking at the lightning bugs and sighing deeply. His eyelids have sunk a bit, and his dewlaps droop, making him look more bloodhoundy than beagley, but I'd never bring it up. Someday, I could be droopy, too. I doubt it, but it could happen.

"Ringer, I am a melancholy dog this long white evening," said John the Beagle. "I was just thinking that—sorry. Baaayouuuuuuuuuu!" He threw his head back and bayed at the moon with all his strength, a lovely sight. When he had finished, I complimented him.

"You are the Pavarotti of the backyard," I said. "You sound like the Three Tenors singing 'Nessun dorma!' from *Turandot* by Puccini. I salute you."

"Wish I had the appetite of the Three Tenors," he said. "You want that soup bone?" He pointed to a humped shadow in the grass. "I've had it for three days, just can't get interested in things of the flesh. Perhaps I can enlighten you about something this fine evening?"

"Actually, I'm writing a book about the Millennium, and I was specifically interested in all the medical discoveries that have taken place lately, with things like cancer and impotence."

"Human men," he sighed. "Is there a sorrier species? When Nature says they can, they run wild; and when Nature says they can't, they go wild in the laboratory. Now they can go wild again. Why doesn't somebody make a pill that makes men think? You know why?"

"Why?"

"Because they'd only sell about eight of them worldwide in the *next* thousand years," said John the Beagle.

"Well, with all your vast reading and learning, can you tell me anything about what new drugs might be coming in the first decade of the New Millennium?" I asked. "It might be something good for my book."

"Let me see," he said. He stood and walked a few feet, scratched with his hind feet and bayed a bit. He growled, mrfed, wagged his tail, and coughed.

"What was all that about?"

"Just going through the whole repertoire before I sit down to think," he said. "I know you don't really understand dogs, Ringer, any more than I understand cats."

"What's to understand about cats?" I said. "We're warm, friendly, lovable, and intelligent. We are companions and friends. Except for

37

colors and the length of our fur, we all look pretty much alike. But dogs? You go from yappy little chihuahuas like Chico to mastiffs. What are we supposed to make of that? You're all over the board."

"My small furry friend, you misunderstand us, and perhaps you misunderstand the Millennium as well," said John the Beagle. "We have evolved over the centuries in shapes that suit our usefulness. We can do many things, from rooting out vermin, a specialty of mine, to guarding sheep, to working as guide dogs for the blind. Have you ever heard of a guide cat? You should be more humble about your limitations, Ringer."

"Well, that's neither here nor there. Tell me about drugs in this New Millennium."

John licked his right foot for a few moments, obviously deep in contemplation. I waited for what he would say. The lightning bugs sang those buggy rounds they sing—did you know they sing in rounds? If I hear "Row, Row, Row Your Boat" one more time from lightning bugs, I'm going to hurl.

"Okay, here's how I see it, Ringer," began John. "I won't go into the usual diseases, but here are some new cures I see from my vast reading. Well, at least as far as "Piranha" through "Scurfy." First, I foresee a complete cure for Newtonism."

"Newtonism?"

"Yes, a dread disease that male and female humans have, makes them speak in unnaturally high voices and wander through casinos in Las Vegas for nights on end. They also tend to smoke and gamble away all the money they have saved in the credit union. Named for Wayne Newton."

"Wow, that's scary," I admitted. "I've never even heard of Newtonism. What else?"

"I predict a new medicine that will put freckles into complete remission," he said, nose nobly up in the air. "This terrible condition, Dorisdayism, afflicts millions around the globe. One woman in Canberra even went mad and used a Bic Banana to join all her freckles like a dot-to-dot puzzle. I believe the condition is either inherited or caused by repeated watchings of Opie on reruns of *The Andy Griffith Show*. Either way, I foresee a new medicine to help it."

"I hadn't known of Dorisdayism," I marvelled. "Modern medicine is really wonderful. What else?"

He stood and scratched his ear and sighed, then ruffed up and ran to the edge of the yard, barked, then came back. I didn't even ask—dogs do that stuff all the time. Maybe even they don't know why.

"I foresee a coming cure for Cicconitis," he intoned. "This terrible disorder makes a person do absolutely *anything* for attention. Named after Madonna's real last name, Ciccone. The person who gets it usually has very little talent except for marketing, and so you often find massive egos in people who have no reason even to be proud. I foresee a single pill that will make a person as useless as, say, Bill Clinton."

"Modern medicine is amazing!" I cried. "And this is all because of the coming Millennium?"

"And finally, I must report with deep satisfaction that I believe there is a coming cure for the Gingr-Itch," he said solemnly.

"No!" I gasped. "How could that be?"

"This condition, as you know, Ringer, causes pompous overblown windbags to seek high office and believe themselves beloved when in fact they are despised," said John the Beagle. "A man can, say, be quietly teaching at a college, but when he contracts the Gingr-Itch, he will start making pronouncements on everything from politics to food supplies. If elected, a person with Gingr-Itch will be whiny, petulant, and yet somehow charismatic, until he collapses in a messy pile of power-grabbing and overweening pride. And then he runs for president. It's a sad thing to see."

"I'll say," I said. "I mean, we animals have fleas and ticks and kennel cough, but at least we don't have the Gingr-Itch. It would be more than any of us could bear."

"Precisely, my boy," he intoned.

I went home thinking a great deal on these coming medical marvels. (I also tried to drag off John the Beagle's soup bone, but after a hundred feet I gave up. Cat teeth aren't made for anything heavy.) When I last saw John, he was looking sadly at the moon and reciting some Keats.

I got home late and let myself in the dog door and went into the bedroom where Mollie and Jerry were sleeping. I jumped softly up on the bed and lay down on Mollie's feet and began to take my bath. Yum, yum! Nothing like a bath after wandering around the neighborhood. I had already started to purr when I heard Mollie's soft voice.

"Ringer? That you? Come up here." She held up her hand, and I eagerly walked up her legs and flopped over in front of her chest so she could rub me. "I hate being away from home. Have you been looking after things?"

"Sure," I said. She sat up as if she had been poked with a cattle prod.

"What??!!!! Did you say something?" she cried. Jerry sat up and asked if something was on fire. "I swear to God, Ringer just talked to me!" Jerry looked at his wife with deep confusion and sighed.

"What did he say?" he asked. Man, was this close! You never *speak* around your humans.

"I asked him if he had been looking after things, and he said '*sure*,'" she said. "I swear, he said it!" Jerry leaned over and looked at me very closely. I purred, hanging on to my best behavior.

"Say something, cat," he said.

"Meeooooowww," I said. Jerry looked sadly at his wife.

"Mollie, you've got to get a grip," he said. He fell back over and soon was snoring loudly.

Mollie started rubbing me again, O bliss.

"You *did* say something didn't you?" she begged. I wanted to say something else, but I knew I couldn't. I had much to think about. It wasn't long until the Millennium—maybe *that* would be the time for all us animal persons to speak.

Chapter Nine

I'm thinking of a color. Can you guess what it is? I'll even give you some to choose from:

   A. Puce
   B. Metallic gray
   C. Lavendar
   D. Purple Haze
   E. The color of Bart Simpson's hair
   F. Yellow streak
   G. Punk black

And the answer? Orange! Never trust a cat! But honestly, some people think interest in ESP, the paranormal, and UFOs will rise to a screaming peak when the New Millennium comes in. Maybe a UFOlet with huge doe eyes and a mild disposition will appear and read the minds of the cast from *The X Files* and, finding nothing there, move on to Washington—what a mistake!

More likely, the guy from space will wind up on *Oprah*, and she'll talk to him about his childhood and whether or not he can forgive somebody—anybody—for something—anything—ever done to him in his life. I'm almost getting the sniffles thinking about it! Maybe Barbara Walters will ask him what kind of mineral he'd like to be.

Reminds me of the time me and some of the cats hereabouts tried to read each other's minds. I'd been reading about the research at Duke University on the subject, and I thought I could lead a fruitful discussion. Which just goes to show something. It was me, Snowball, Larry, and a black cat named Boomer.

"Wait a dern minute," growled Boomer. He was a sorry sight, with one ear almost missing and scars everywhere. "You talking about reading what we're thinking?"

"Sure, like picking out a color or a number," I said.

"I'd rather play Pictionary or cards," whined Snowball.

"You *can't* play Pictionary," said Larry. "You don't have a thumb. You can't draw." Snowball began to look at her paws and then— big surprise—began to take a bath.

"Okay, I'm thinking of a number between one and ten," I said. Boomer had a coughing fit and then washed his face a bit.

"Man, I'm ready to get fixed," he complained. "The way I'm living? It's killing me, I tell you, it's killing me."

"Seven," said Larry.

"Wrong, it was three," I said.

"Oh, oh, I'm thinking of a color between one and ten," said Snowball. Larry and Boomer looked at each other and shrugged.

"Snowball, there's no such thing as a color between one and ten," I said.

"Oh, oh, I meant to say I'm thinking of a number between pink and green!" she cried exultantly.

"That's different," said Boomer, growling a bit. "The answer is six."

"You're making fun of me," said Snowball.

"Maybe I won't need to get fixed after all," said Boomer. "In fact, I might hike to a monastery after listening to this." We finally gave up, though Larry and I took a walk to look for bugs, and on the way we played that ESP game, and neither of us ever got it right.

So, this morning, everybody left. Mollie took the kids to school and then she was going to her hair salon. She kept looking at me oddly, and I'd rub on her legs and make all kinds of routine cat sounds. I decided to see if I could do some ESP experiments with Chico. But then I found out he was asleep under a magnolia tree, and no matter what I said, he'd only grunt and roll over. Dogs. What a useless species.

So, I decided you were about ready for another test, so sharpen those pencils again and get ready for another Thinking Cat Test! Concentrate. Don't worry. Unlike the SAT, the rest of your life doesn't hang in the balance.

Ringer's ESP Test

1. You are at a séance. The medium cries out for the spirit of River Phoenix to appear and speak. What is the best thing for you to do?

>>A. Go to a nightclub and have a Long Island Iced Tea.

>>B. Try to go with the flow.

>>C. Call out his name and ask him what roles he's gotten "over there."

>>D. Give him the current prices of beef futures on the Chicago Mercantile Exchange.

2. If you were able to contact the spirit of Harry Houdini through ESP, what do you think he would say?

>>A. "Tie me up, whip me, beat me."

>>B. "Even though I was of German extraction, I did not then or ever intend to defame any Italians or Italian Americans by use of the name "Houdini," and if anyone has taken offense, I apologize."

>>C. "Get me out of here, I'm drowning!"

>>D. "If you're going to saw one woman
in half, let it be Shania Twain."

**3. If you could read Martha Stewart's mind, you'd see she
was ...**

>>A. Thinking about ways to short-cir-
cuit all of Bob Vila's tools.

>>B. Aghast at how poorly your eyes
match your shoes.

>>C. Chanting the mantra "*Kmart, money;
Kmart, money; Kmart, money.*"

>>D. Thinking of running for president
of the United States on the Plaid
Party.

**4. You run into Michael Flatley, formerly of "Lord of the
Dance," and he takes you by the shoulders and stares in
your eyes. What is he thinking?**

>>A. That you don't appreciate—*can't*
appreciate—that he is the greatest
dancer in the world and you are
nobody.

>>B. That if his pants were tighter he
could sing soprano.

>>C. The number five.

>>D. That Riverdance is nothing without
him and that you'd better admit it
or he'll do a jig on your instep.

**5. Now concentrate on this one. Don't get fooled! I, Ringer
McGee, am thinking of three people who have failed in
their careers. Who are they?**

>>A. Eric Roberts, Bill Clinton, and Bob
Novak.

>>B. Michael Bolton, "Do" of the
Heaven's Gate cult, and Bob Novak.

>>C. Roberto Alomar, John Major, and Bob
Novak.

>>D. Pee-Wee Herman, Billy Ray Cyrus,
and Bob Novak.

**6. Which president of the United States are we most likely
to reach through ESP and why?**

>>A. Abraham Lincoln, because his great
    mind expands to fill the entire
    universe with its compassion and
    justice.

>>B. Richard Nixon because he's out in
    the cosmos whistling for Checkers.

>>C. John F. Kennedy because he and
    Marilyn are sitting around a celes-
    tial pool having cocktails.

>>D. George Bush for no particular
    reason.

Time's up! Put your pencils down and pass your paper to the
person in front of you and get ready for a career where the question you'll ask most is "Can I supersize that?"

Chapter Ten

Mollie got home and decided to watch some TV, and I curled up on the arm of her chair and looked at her carefully, like a cat. She was watching a rerun of *Little House on the Prairie*, and I had to get ready, because she always bawls when Laura does something sweet or Michael Landon tosses his hair. (Actually she cries every time she sees Michael Landon, since he died.)

So I was watching it with her, and it was an episode where Laura thinks nobody loves her and she runs away, and she's in all kinds of hideous trouble. And I'm thinking, yeah, and the Santa Monica Freeway's just over the hill, when suddenly Mollie picked me up and looked me in the eye.

"I *know* you spoke to me last night," she said. "I know it. Do it again. Say something. Come on, Ringer."

"Meow," I said.

"Don't *meow* me, buster," she said. She shook me a little. I *loved* that. I didn't like being called Buster—that cat is an idiot. I began to purr—couldn't help it. Love that gal! "Ringer, what's going on?"

Then she set me down and did something I had never seen before: She actually turned off an episode of *Little House on the Prairie* just as everybody was about to hug and wail. She rolled me over on my back and leaned down. Mollie's a doll, but no cat likes a human this close. I struggled a little, but she held me tighter.

"Hello, furball, I'm talking to you," she said. "Are you dense? Are you an idiot? Hello in there, Ringer McGee. Say something." An idiot? This was getting personal.

"Meee—eee—yow," I said. Sometimes people think an extra syllable means something.

She turned her head. This meow thing clearly wasn't working, and I wasn't sure what my next delaying tactic might be.

"One word, Ringer," she said. "Just say one word. Say *cat* or *dog* or *Mollie*."

I should pause here and repeat something: ALL us animals have a vow never to talk to our humans. Never. Ever. Word gets around that an animal's going to break the vow? He winds up on the fender of a Peugeot. We'll scruff and scratch and say it was too bad, but we saw it coming. Sort of like a fat guy who has the Big One while trying to steal second at the company softball game. So I'd already plopped one paw in the grave by saying *sure* to Mollie. Actually speaking to her seemed completely out of the question.

"Mrf, prrrrrrrr," I said, standing on her lap and arching my back. Not Michael Landon, but not bad.

"Wait! I know what this is!" she said with a gasp. She stood, and I slid to the floor and looked up at her, trying to parse this latest turn of events. If I played this right, I might get a piece of bacon or a twist-tie out of Mollie for my cooperation. Mollie put her hands on her forehead and nodded as if she'd suddenly been given a great insight.

"Meow," I said encouragingly.

"This is happening because it's the beginning of the New Millennium!" she cried. I backed up and felt like I might hack up a hairball. The room felt small and airless. I needed some fresh air. Or maybe I'd just go hide in the litter box. Nobody ever followed me there. "That's it, isn't it, Ringer? When the Millennium comes, all the animals will begin to talk!"

This was hideous, like finding out your favorite aunt embezzled money from an orphan's home. Mollie had gone New Age on me. And it was mostly my fault.

"Meeeeeooooooowww!" I cried desperately. I ran into the kitchen hoping to change the subject. Mollie doesn't like me in the kitchen because I tend to annoy her when she cooks and also I once ate a magnet that fell off the refrigerator, thinking it was a bug. Cost Jerry $318 to have it surgically removed from me at the vet. I also tend to lick the tub of butter when she leaves it out. Of course, it also makes me barf, so nobody's too happy.

"Don't give me that *meow* junk," Mollie said. She poured herself a cup of Starbuck's Sumatra from the Krups and leaned against the sink and watched me. I jumped on the counter, sniffing for butter or for some way out. "You think I'm an idiot, don't you, Ringer? You think you can speak a word of English to me, and I'll just assume I'm having a breakdown and need a Xanax. Well, you've got another thing coming!"

This was serious. She was starting to talk to me like she did to Buck and Annie. Actually the only thing I had coming was how to escape. I could run away and hide. Let's face it, people have no ability to hide. Cats? You could give me a fifteen-minute head start, and the entire FBI, CIA, and even a special prosecutor couldn't find me. I couldn't run from Mollie, though. She was my person. I needed to think. I concentrated: Think, Ringer, think! Maybe I could fake an injury. That wasn't bad. Except she'd take me to that sawbones veterinarian. The first thing he always does is take my temperature with a cattle prod. Nooooo thank you. Or I could start growling and run through Chico's door and disappear into the ferns. Sometimes I lie in ferns all day napping or scarfing up a few roly-polys.

"You're probably thinking of what you're going to do next, aren't you?" she said. This was getting scary. Maybe I should ask her to pick a color between one and ten. I sat down on the counter and stared into the burners. Sometimes a Yummy Thing will get dropped in there, but I have to be hungry to go after it. "Don't look in there, you're just changing the subject."

Just then, like a plot device from a John Grisham novel, the phone rang. It was Mollie's editor calling from New York, so I took the opportunity to flee outside and go sit under the magnolia tree. The day was hot, the kind I like, and soon I was somewhere between sleepy and woozy. I lay down in some nice dirt, and soon I fell asleep.

Then I had the following dream.

Chapter Eleven

I'm standing in a field, and there's a small house with smoke feathering up from a single chimney. Suddenly Michael Landon runs past me, being chased by Mollie, who's holding a crystal.

"Talk to me!" Mollie yells. "Talk to me!"

Suddenly the door of the Little House opens and Bob Vila steps out and yells that the concert's about to start, so I saunter over there and go inside, and Michael Bolton is standing next to the fireplace, and Barry Manilow is playing the piano for him! I can't hang around for *this*, so I step back outside and find Barbra Streisand and Sally Field wrestling in what appears to be a vat of tapioca.

Barbra raises up long enough to shriek at me and tell me that I don't deserve even to *hear* "Stony End" again. Before I can gag, Sally smiles brilliantly and says. "You like me! You really like me!" This is a terrible dream.

I hotfoot it past the house and into the edge of the woods, hoping to find Mollie and Michael Landon, when Tristan D'Amore and Pierre Du Pint suddenly confront me and ask me to speak.

"I can't!" I cry. "It's not allowed!"

"Ah, small friend, you *can* speak after all," says Tristan.

"Get him to do Nixon's "Checkers" speech," says Pierre.

I run away from them into the woods, and suddenly I'm in a verdent glen, surrounded by members of the Heaven's Gate cult doing, apparently, an interpretative dance to "You Light Up My Life" by Debby Boone. They invite me to join them in the quadrille and sarabande, and I flee screaming through the forest, but I hear footsteps behind me and glance back to see I am being chased by Yanni and John Tesh. But I outrun them, and finally I am lying beside a huge waterfall, breathing hard, even panting, my tongue hanging out like a small, wet, pink ribbon.

I feel a bit hazy and exhausted, and only after a few minutes do I realize that Uri Geller is sitting in a chair not ten feet away bending spoons and throwing each new one on to a huge pile. He seems very sad.

"What's wrong?" I ask.

"Is this all there is?" he says.

Then I'm running again, and there's a giant running beside me, with shoes the size of a Volkswagen, and I look up, higher and higher and higher and see that it's a Giant Mollie, and she's pointing at me and her mouth opens, and this voice like thunder in the Himalayas falls to me, heavy and accusing.

"Speak . . . to . . . me!" it booms. "I . . . know . . . you talk!" With each word, trees fall down, and I tumble in the grass. Men are burning pyres to keep the Giant Mollie away, threatening her with spears and throwing empty Perrier bottles.

"Meow?" I offer.

Then she stops and suddenly her foot is rising up, and there's this malevolent look on her face, like the pleased sadism of a James Bond villain. And now her foot is coming down, and I know she means to stomp me about thirty feet into the ground, and so I scream:

"Don't do it, Mollie! You'll regret it—maybe not today, maybe not tomorrow, but soon, and for the rest of your life!" But she stomps down anyway with the torque of planets. Wham!

Suddenly, I awoke beneath the magnolia tree, gasping for air, trying to see if I was in one piece. A squirrel named Bob stood near me watching with great interest. Squirrels are idiots.

"Good grief, what a hideous dream!" I said.

"You was dancing, Ringer," said Bob. "I sorter liked it."

"Don't you have a nut to peel or something?" I asked acidly.

"You kept mewling and talking and dancing and running," he said. "I thought it was, uh, funny. Hee."

I got up and stretched, still feeling a bit disoriented and shaky. Poor Bob. Sometimes you have to realize people are just doing the best they can.

"Show's over now, Bob," I said. "Besides, don't you remember that cats eat squirrels?"

"Oh yeah, you do, well, I be dog," he said.

"You be *squirrel*, Bob," I sighed. He climbed a tree then went to a mud puddle and drank for a long time. I was in big trouble, but I could not let it deter me from my search for the truth about the Millennium. The bad news now was that Mollie was looking for it too.

Chapter Twelve

It's 3 A.M. and I'm trying to type quietly on Mollie's computer. I hid from her most of the evening, in fact I stayed with Annie in her room. She dressed me up in Raggedy Anne clothes and rocked me while we watched *South Park* together. Buck came in one time, but Annie threw him out. Sure, I feel like an idiot as Raggedy Anne, but it's better than Mollie chasing me and asking me to talk.

Tonight, in this quiet study, I'm going to go farther than I have before. I am going to become Nostraringermus, prophet.

Specifically, I am going to make some political predictions based on the positions of the planets and astrological signs. I can't sleep anyway. Don't want to be chased anymore by Yanni and John Tesh.

♒ 1. Prediction number one:
Saturn enters Aquarius.

From this I foresee a radical change in administrations. I predict a new group called the Free Beer Party will arise from the ashes of the Democrats, or what's left of them. This party, led by a senator from North Carolina who was previously best known for hating everything, will promise free beer to everybody over the age of 21, along with a ticket to a NASCAR race of their choice. (Snooty New Yorkers can trade in the NASCAR ticket for a wine and cheese party hosted by Susan Sontag.)

♒ 2. Prediction number two:
Aquarius enters Uranus.

Quit snickering. You're acting like a teenager. The Anti-Free Beer Party will arise almost simultaneously, with Ralph Reed as party chairman. Instead of free beer, every member of this party will be given a hair shirt and a subscription to The Wall Street Journal. *Party members won't know that Reed is also a paid consultant for the Free Beer Party.*

♉ 3. Prediction number three:
Pluto enters Taurus.

Who knew a Disney dog wanted to drive a Ford? Just kidding. Ross Perot will announce that he has bought Steve Forbes and will dress him in livery and make him learn to play the accordian. Together

they will run the I Got Plenty of Nothing Party, which will promise to eliminate taxes, force everyone to listen to Elton John songs until they can understand what he is saying, and support an invasion of Canada.

 4. Prediction number four:
Mercury enters Scorpio.

Ralph Nader will form the Killjoy Party, which is against everything. This party will promote the elimination of cars, houses, and smiling. Everything will be painted green because "it is the color of life."

 5. Prediction number five:
Mars enters Sagittarius.

The Womyn's Party, Dammit will be started by Susan Faludi, Andrea Dworkin, and Gloria Steinem. No men will be allowed in The Womyn's Party, Dammit. This party will support the deportation of all men to Devil's Island, and Camille Paglia too, if she doesn't toe the line! The Womyn's Party, Dammit will not tolerate anything. My way or the highway!

 6. Prediction number six:
Neptune enters Leo.

Seventy-four million Americans will join in a mass enclave to form the Victim's Party. To join, you just have to prove that you are a victim and aren't responsible for anything you do or might have done in the past. Victimhood can be based on anything and you don't have to prove anything either. If you say you are a victim, it is assumed you are a victim.

Now, a lot of people might not believe in the conjunction of the planets and the astrological signs, particularly when it comes to political parties. Those people have obviously been thinking too much. What will they believe in next? Science? Sheesh.

I myself was born under the sign of Aquarius (like you didn't know already!) which means I am creative, loyal, and like fried foods. Here are a few astrological signs and how I predict you will act during the change to the New Millennium:

Taurus. You bulls have always tended to vote Republican, but after 2000 I believe you will vote independent, start wearing flare jeans, and become Natalie Merchant fans. You will form a loose coalition with the people in the Free Beer Party until you make fools of yourselves at a party and beg Ralph Reed to lead you out of your wickedness. Ralph's company says they'll do it for $418,000, whereupon you'll take up Marlboros and watch old Dean Martin movies.

Leo. The Millennium will be a strange time for you lions. First of all, you will all join a pyramid scheme involving miniature golf and a certain gentleman from Colombia. Before you know it, you'll be in over your heads with windmills, dinosaurs, and the DEA. You'll sell your shares before any real damage is done and become stable boys and girls for Merv Griffin Enterprises.

Scorpio. You cash in! All Scorpios will rise to the top in every political organization, becoming ward captains, block chiefs, and Petty Underlings, the latter being a new category instigated by Republicans for everybody who doesn't give more than ten grand a year to the party. With your newfound wealth and power, you will discriminate against others not like you, join a country club, and take up smoking cigars.

Aquarius. Bad news, Aquarians. Your fortunes will fall after the Millennium, and you will probably form your own party called The Used-to-Haves. You will whine so much that even the Victim's Party won't have you! You will all drive Pintos, Yugos, and Ramblers, and no Scorpios will invite you to parties at the club. You will work as house servants even for the Petty Underlings.

Sagittarius. You will all be members of the I-Got-Plenty-of-Nothing Party and will work for Ross Perot and Steve Forbes at minimum wage, which by 2005 will have been lowered by Republicans to fifty cents a week. You will be forced to listen to lectures by Perot, in which he rambles about sinister forces which are trying to invade his precious bodily fluids.

Pisces. First, you join the Green Party and organize the March Against Ozone, but only eighteen people turn out and you're fired. After that, you turn socialist and promote a doctor-pupil ratio of 1:1. The AMA comes out in favor of you. You decide to run for president, but the National Rifle Association shoots you down. You spend nine months recovering from your wounds at the Betty Ford Clinic.

♎ Libra. The Millennium will lead you to renounce things of the flesh. Your husband asks for a divorce.

♊ Gemini. You help form the Disco Party and nominate Donna Summer for president. Your motto is "Unzip the Unhip!" and Bill Clinton agrees to speak at your convention.

♋ Cancer. You join the Libertarian Party and support the elimination of all laws. You also dismantle the armed forces. In three years, we are invaded by Panama and made to pay reparations for "that Canal thing."

♑ Capricorn. The Millennium will bring you to a new understanding of your own life and that of others. You will be kind, decent, and fair. You will never lie. No political party will have you.

♈ Aries. You are all Democrats, but you sell your mailing list to the Petty Underlings, for whom you feel sorry. The Underlings then launch an all-out attack against you. You take the side of the Underlings in the battle. When they have you all cornered in Montana, you offer them block grants if they will call off the attack. They accept the block grants and then blow you to pieces. Survivors send a letter of apology to the Petty Underling leaders.

♍ Virgo. You fall in with a group of anti-government survivalists who print their own money and refuse to pay taxes.

You set up a home shopping channel to sell painted terra-cotta chihuahuas.

Whew, I'm worn out, it's nearly 3 A.M., and soon the Krups will crank up in the kitchen. If Mollie ever finds these files, I'm cooked. Maybe I ought to think about spilling the beans to her. Maybe it's time to get rid of this burden.

Chapter Thirteen

You won't believe the day I've had. I went into the laundry room and climbed into the dryer and slept on Buck's shirts for a couple of hours before I awoke just as Jerry was leaving. He was telling Mollie and the kids about a woman who was allergic to her husband.

"What'd you tell her to do?" asked Mollie.

"Bury him in the backyard," said Jerry, sipping his coffee. Buck had a choking fit he laughed so hard.

"Dad, that's really sick," said Annie. I was just passing through, and I escaped into the yard. Rain fell pleasantly over the neighborhood, straight down with no wind, and I felt relieved to get out of the house. I sauntered around a while, then went down to Larry's house, where I found the traitor snuggling up with Snowball at the base of a gardenia bush.

"Ahem," I said, and they both jumped.

"Ringer—hey!" said Larry, clearing his throat. "I was just discussing with Snowball which moths taste bad. She'd bit into a luna moth, and it gave her a migraine."

"I bet, " I said.

"Heeyyyy, Ringeeerrrrrrr," said Snowball, arching over to rub against me. Sometimes I hate being a male. Our brains fail us at the worst times. "Somebody was talking about you yesterday."

"Who? Who was talking about me?" I asked.

"Gin-gerrrrr James," said Mollie. "She said you had a fine strut. And I said, 'Why Ginger James, you know very well that Ringer McGee has a fine strut! Everybody in the neighborhood knows about that boy's strut!'" Larry rolled over into the grass, laughing.

Just then, a new cat I'd never seen came prancing up, and we all smelled each other, touched noses, made the ritual introductions. Her name was (ack) Fluffy, a black cat with dark blue eyes. I expected another Snowball.

"I guess you're just wandering around looking for guys," I said. She came very close and looked me in the eyes and smiled.

"Yeah, and I'll let you know if I see any," said Fluffy. Larry was giggling again. "I was just tired of reading and came outside for a stretch."

"What were you reading? Danielle Steele?" I asked. My voice was edgy. This wasn't starting well.

"Actually, I'm halfway through *The Decline of the West* by Oswald Spengler," she said. "But I could read a Danielle Steele book if you want me to tell you the plot." Wow! I was starting to like her better by the minute. Not only was she well read, but she had wit and sass.

"I want to get back to this, but I need to talk to Larry in private if I can," I said.

"There's some over there," said Snowball, pointing with her nose. "Some private bushes," said Snowball. Larry and I looked at each other.

"*Privet*," I said, "Not *private*. Snowball, you never cease to amaze me."

"Oh, thanks," she said demurely. "Hee."

Larry and I walked about a hundred feet away and sat beneath a tulip poplar. The rain was coming down hard now, so we made a dash to a nearby porch and went under it. The smell was dusty, and it was very quiet. I liked it. I was going to take one major nap later in the day.

"What?" asked Larry. "What's this Secret Agent Man stuff?"

"I've got a big problem," I admitted. "I said a word in front of Mollie." Larry sat on his haunches and looked out at the rain.

"Then I'm going to have to rip your throat out," he said mildly. "You know the code."

"It was an accident," I spluttered. "She'd been gone away on book tour, and she was rubbing me, and I was just glad to see her."

"What word did you say?"

"I said the word *sure*. She asked me a question and I said *sure*."

"Not exactly 'Mr. Watson, come here, I want you' is it?" he said.

"No," I said miserably. "And what's worse, she thinks it's an early sign of the change in the Millennium. That all animals are going to start talking." Larry started taking a bath, which irritated me. He stopped from time to time.

"Ringer, you've screwed up before, and you'll screw up again," said Larry. "It's your nature."

"Wait, you idiot, that's a line from *Body Heat*," I scolded. Larry and I sometimes watch movies together. My all-time favorite is *That Darn Cat*. Sue me, I like old Disney movies. "At least be original in your condemnation."

"Well, this is it," he said. "We're sending you over, babe."

"And that's from *The Maltese Falcon*!" I shouted, waving my paws at him for effect. He didn't seem to be threatened. "What's next, *Gone With the Wind*?"

"Ringer, you're getting hysterical," Larry said. "Calm down. It was just an incident. Look at her like she's lost her mind when she tries to get you to do it again. It's no big deal. If it gets worse, let me know, and I'll arrange to have a piano dropped on you."

"Thanks a lot."

"No problem. Didn't you just hate that Fluffy chick?" he asked, shuddering.

"Actually, I kind of liked her," I said. "I'm getting tired of Snowball. That girl's dumb as a stump."

"Yeah, but she's great for smooching in the bushes," said Larry.

"I'm going to take a walk," I said. "I'll catch you later."

"Later, man."

And so I went out into the rain with a lot on my mind. What if it was true? What if all us animals were going to start talking when the Millennium changed? At first, it would be a novelty. Barbara Walters would interview an Alsatian. Geraldo would talk to a wallaby about what makes him so jumpy. People would expect things of us. And as we all know, cats never do anything they don't feel like. Perhaps the entire world as we animals knew it was going into the litter box.

Nah.

Chapter Fourteen

When I got home, Mollie was gone and the house was quiet. I let myself inside and read some of *Gravity's Rainbow* by Thomas Pynchon. There weren't any cats in it, but I liked it anyway. Finally, I dozed off for a few hours on top of Mollie's computer and thankfully didn't dream anything about Barbra Streisand or crystals. This Millennium thing was really starting to weigh on my mind.

Nothing better than a long nap on a rainy day. When I awoke, I found Mollie sitting next to me wearing a striped shirt and polka-dotted pants. She'd never go out that way, so she'd been home for a while. People's taste in private is really appalling. Then again, the very idea of clothing is so hilarious to animals that we joke about it all the time. Creatures without body hair or fur are kind of pathetic. There's a Chinese crested chihuahua named Ming two blocks over. Looks like something that caught on fire and got stomped out with track shoes.

So I sat up and yawned and smacked my lips a little and looked around. The kids weren't home yet, so it wasn't after four. I was going to watch Turner Classic Movies for a while, but I'd waited too late. Drat. Mollie was giving me that look. What did I do now?

"Come on Ringer," she said urgently. She rubbed me, and my back went up higher than the St. Louis Gateway arch. Can't fight nature. "You know we're best friends? Haven't I always been your best friend?" She had me there. I adored Mollie, and she treated me like King Ringer the Bold. "If we're best friends, why don't you just go ahead and say something again? I know you're the smartest cat in the world."

She was good. She was very, very good. (Oops—that's a line Indiana Jones used to describe the French archaeologist Belloc in *Raiders of the Lost Ark*.) But what would happen to me and all animals if I broke the code? I had only heard of one animal in Athens breaking the code before, a slobbery St. Bernard named Happy who lived with some University of Georgia students. They kept putting beer in his bowl.

One night, this Happy, drunk and drooling said, aloud, "Bring me a keg, Nigel, for I have needs of sustenance." I have no idea where the oaf got the line, but it sounds like an old Sidney Greenstreet movie. Anyway, the students went mad, called the local papers and a TV station, and when they came, Happy had sobered up. Nobody thought it was funny. Happy disappeared mysteriously, and there were rumors he'd been "erased," though he may have followed a hot poodle off.

But never mind. My point is still clear. I think.

"Come on, Ringer, say something to me." I suddenly felt madly impulsive and was glad I wasn't watching the Home Shopping Network. What is the worst that could happen? She would probably smile at me, hug me, and say that she loved me even more! I could swear Mollie to secrecy! Everything was going to be all right!

"Just one word, Ringer," she cooed. She picked me up and held my head against her face. O bliss. I turned and put my mouth next to her ear.

"Okay, but you've got to promise not to kiss and tell," I said.

Mollie exploded. Or that's how it seemed to me. She threw me across the room where I banged into Jerry's golf clubs. I tried to grab on to his Big Bertha, but it was too slippery. I crashed. Mollie threw her arms up and ran screaming through the house, probably the second most hideous sound I've ever heard. (The worst was when Snowball caught her tail in a Weedeater.) Mollie seemed terrified, I was addled, and this was clearly panic time.

I decided to follow her. She was in the kitchen huddled against the counter where the Cuisinart sat like a squat robot. When she saw me, she jumped backward on the counter, seat first.

"You get near me, I'll throw a knife, I swear to God!" she screamed. "This isn't happening! This isn't happening!" She pointed at me as if that might keep me, the Creature from the Black Lagoon, at bay.

"Mollie, cats can jump on counters," I said mildly.

"You jump up here, and I'll cut your head off with a spoooon!" she screamed. Then, to herself, she said, "I've got to call 911. If I could just get to a phone and call 911! And the kids will be here any minute!" She began to sniffle a little and whined miserably, "My house has turned into *Poltergeist!*"

"Mollie, please calm down," I said. I jumped up on the counter across the kitchen from her near the stove. Hmmm. Something smelled good up here. "You've been begging me to talk, and now that I have, you're acting like a ninny. Let's act like two mature people."

"You're not a people!" she shrieked. "You're an evil spirit!" She gasped and put her hand on her chest. "Are you Death?" I started laughing—couldn't help it.

"Nah, Death is a chihuahua," I said. I thought it was pretty funny, but she didn't laugh. "Let's talk this out." I started to walk toward her around the counters. She threw a loaf of honey bran bread at me, but I dodged it easily.

"I thought it was because of the Millennium, but now I realize I'm just going crazy," Mollie said. "That's it, isn't it? I'm a fruitcake? But wait, I can't tell anybody. I'll just have to try and act normal. Act normal?!!! With Death in my house?"

"I'm not Death," I said, exasperated. "He wears a black robe."

"I don't believe it," she said. "You're Death. I never believed he wore a black robe and carried a sickle."

"A *scythe*," I corrected. "Death carries a scythe. Nobody but a savage would carry a sickle." She snuffled out a laugh before she went marble-eyed again. Maybe I was getting somewhere. "Mollie, look, animals can talk. We read while you're gone, and we watch TV just like you do. It's our secret, because we're afraid if they knew people would, well, scream and jump on kitchen counters and stuff like that."

"Poor Annie and Buck, their mother's gone around the bend," said Mollie. "Now how can I get off this counter so it won't get me?" She looked around for a weapon but could only find a spatula from a plastic container behind the Cuisinart.

"You're going to attack me with a spatula?" I said in mock horror. "I'll get some tongs and we can fight to the death." This time she laughed out loud.

"You're Death," she said. "But you're pretty funny."

She slid off the counter with the spatula, brandishing it at me like Zorro. I jumped down after her, and she ran in the den and leaped, feet first, on to the couch. She waved her implement menacingly.

"That's probably the proper weapon if you want to attack a burger," I said, sitting on the carpet before her. "But it's no way to confront a man."

"You're not a man!!" she cried. "You're an evil spirit! Evil Ringer! You've probably been around since medieval times scaring women and taunting old men! Wait—I need an exorcist. I could get him to come and get you out of my house. But wait—my head might start turning around any minute and the room's going to become freezing cold."

"Mollie, that was a movie," I said. "Directed by William Friedkin. Linda Blair. The voice of Mercedes McCambridge. I'm a movie buff. Ask me a question." She calmed down a minute. I'd seen most of my movies in her lap, after all. She lowered the spatula and glared at me.

"Who directed *Tender Mercies*?" she asked.

"Bruce Beresford," I said.

"What was the name of Faye Dunaway's character in *Chinatown*?"

"Evelyn Mulwray."

"Who played Captain Nemo in *Twenty Thousand Leagues Under the Sea*?"

"James Mason. This could go on all night."

"Well, it doesn't prove anything!" she screamed, waving the spatula again. "You are probably just taunting me if you are Death. But I'm not going! I have a family! I have a husband and two children I love!"

"Your husband sticks needles in people and makes them sneeze," I said. She started laughing hysterically, and I might have won the day, but she heard the school bus stopping on the rainy street out front.

"It's the kids!" she cried. "Ringer, if you say a word to them, so help me, I'll take you ten miles in the country and put you out near a Dumpster."

"Did you know *Dumpster* is a trade name and should be capitalized?" I said. "Don't worry, I won't talk around the kids, Mollie. And you're not crazy. And if the other animals find out I broke the code, they'll throw me in the cage with that pit bull over on Prince Avenue."

"It's the Millennium," she said. "What are we going to do? I've got to get a crystal or something."

"Ack, no crystals, and it's not the Millennium," I said. "It's just me, Mollie. Good old Ringer. Your best friend, remember?"

"Say a word, and you're toast," she said.

"Not even a wry comment if I'm struck by the ultimate sadness of life?" I asked. Wit and sass.

"Shut your mouth!" she warned, and suddenly the front door flew open and Buck and Annie came face to face with their mother standing on the sofa with a spatula.

"This is so cool!" said Buck.

"Mom, what are you doing?" said Annie, somewhat alarmed. Annie looked flushed, a bit panic-stricken. She kept glancing at me. I sat on my haunches, Ringer the Inscrutable.

"I . . . uh, I was trying to kill a fly," she said.

"Cool," said Buck. "With a burger flipper. This is way strange."

"Ringer could catch a fly," said Annie. "He could catch anything. Couldn't you, Ringer?" She threw her book bag on the couch and slid two feet to the floor on her knees and scooped me up. Mollie made a high-pitched, strangling sound far back in her throat. I began to purr, and threw my head back and bumped Annie's cheek.

Mollie cautiously stepped off the sofa and looked at me to make sure I wasn't going to bite Annie's throat. Buck went into the kitchen, and Mollie called him Gerald McGee Junior, and told him to get away from the junk food. Annie took me in her room and dressed me up in doll clothes and pushed me around in a stroller.

Conquering Mollie and the Millennium was going to be harder than I thought.

SAINT RIDGER

Chapter Fifteen

Now what? It's been a screwy couple of days since I spoke to Mollie, and the first day she avoided me entirely even though I did nothing but some precious meowing. She kept looking at me, but every time I'd look back, she'd point her finger at me and leave the room. Today she drove to Atlanta to shop with her sister Katie, who lives in the suburb of Marietta.

I slept all morning. Call me irresponsible. Then I awoke thinking about the Millennium again and how I was going to win Mollie back. At the moment, she thinks I'm a cross between Godzilla and Jean-Paul Sartre—though I know I'm a saint—so this is going to be dicey at best. Then again, there's this computer-glitch problem facing us at the Millennium, so to distract myself, I thought I'd come up with another test.

I had some friends with me, anyway. Snowball, Larry, and Buster were in the back yard, along with the new black cat named Fluffy. I showed them all Chico's dog door, and they trooped right in behind me. Chico started whining and said he was going to call the police, alert the neighborhood watch, etc.

"Chico, go suck some marrow, okay?" said Larry. We all giggled. Chico snorted and huffed and went outside and chewed on a sock. Larry had been in the house before, but the others had not, so I took them on a brief tour. Sure, I was showing off, but living well *is* the best revenge.

I showed them the kids' rooms first, and Annie's room was perfectly neat, with everything in its place. Buck's room looked as if it had been attacked by nineteenth-century British explorers with machetes.

"This is pathetic," said Larry. "I love it! Look at all the places to hide. Hey! Pizza!"

"Wait, don't—" I started, but cats are cats, and soon they were all sampling the remains of a snack from three days before. Yum. I took them into Jerry's and Mollie's room, and Snowball was impressed.

"Ohhhh, Ringggeeerrrr, I could just sit in here on that sunny bed all day, bathing and napping," she said. "Do you have mice? That would be so cool."

"Mice?" said Fluffy. "This house doesn't even have a microbe."

"Oh, uh, the microbe's usually in the kitchen so you can make popcorn," said Snowball. Larry gave me one of his looks. Fluffy raised one eyebrow and shrugged. A voice—Buster's—came from the bathroom.

"Hey, the lid's up! Y'all come get a drink!" he said.

"I'm going to hurl," said Fluffy mildly.

I showed them the rest of the house, and they loved the pool table downstairs. Larry and Buster kicked the balls into the pockets while Snowball praised them ridiculously. I took Fluffy to one side while the boys were acting like boys.

"So, it's nice to find somebody around here who's smart," I said. "You just move in?"

"Three weeks ago," she said. "I haven't been out much. I hate moving. We came here from South Dakota. Lots of reading time up there." This was starting off nicely. "What have you been reading lately?"

"Actually," I admitted, "I've been studying the Millennium. I'm writing a book about it." I thought that would impress her. Instead, she began snickering and then laughing.

"Got your crystal, yet, Ringer?" she asked. "Want me to bring you some jasmine incense and finger cymbals?"

"Hey, I meant—"

"I know what you meant," she said. "You know what? You and all your tie-dyed friends can just kiss my big old poofy tail, because only morons believe the Millennium means anything."

"Hey, I meant—"

"And let's face it, Ringer, the world is mostly full of morons who will believe anything at all," she said. My fur began to bristle along the back of my neck. What the heck was I doing? I had spent days debunking the Millennialists, and here I was, about to take up for them? Go figure. "Hey, don't go getting spiky on me." (That's cat lingo for getting mad.)

"Fluffy—and that's *such* an intellectual name—when was the last time somebody told you that you'd stepped into the wrong territory?" I said. I thought she would argue back at me, which just goes to show what men know about women. She arched her back and hissed at me violently. Larry and Buster stopped kicking pool balls and jumped down, Snowball right behind.

"Kids, kids, can't we have a little healthy recreation?" said Larry. I turned to him and hissed violently. I didn't mean to—just had to. Hissing is catching among cats, like yawning is among people.

"Want me to kill her?" said Buster mildly. "I could tear her throat out."

By then, Fluffy and I were circling each other. What would they do if they knew I'd broken the code and spoken to Mollie? I was feeling rather surly. The more I thought about it, the angrier I got. I wanted to be alone. I wanted to hit the old computer and work on my theories. For a moment, Fluffy let down her guard, and I jumped on her with all fours.

I bit her ears. Hard. I kicked her stomach. She howled and hissed and ran back up the stairs, and I chased her, nipped at her tail, while the others tumbled along, Snowball crying for us to stop and Buster and Larry cheering me on. I chased Fluffy right out Chico's dog door and into the backyard.

"Man, this is fun!" said Larry.

"But what about her *feelings*?" cried Snowball. "What about her *feelings*?"

"If she brings her feelings back in here, I'll scratch their eyes out," said Buster.

"I need some time alone," I said.

"Are you getting in touch with your inner kitten?" said Larry, making each word long and drawn out.

"When was the last time you had your claws pulled out with a Vise-Grip?" I asked.

"Whoa ho," said Larry. "Come on Snowy. I'll catch you some crickets and we can pull their legs off."

"Okay," she said. "I don't want to be around Ringer. He has no manners. I can't stand a cat with no manners."

I herded them all out and sat in the kitchen for a long time, trying to collect myself. What was going on? Whither Ringer? Maybe the Millennium was working its invisible power on me after all. Maybe it was pulling me, like a magnet, into its deep and enduring spell. Perhaps it had been like this in the year 999 when people still thought cats were witches.

Naaahh.

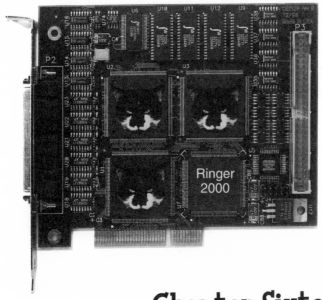

Chapter Sixteen

I went to the computer and turned it on and surfed the Web for a while. Sometimes I get on a chat line. (Did you know *chat* is French for cat?) My search engine told me there were 1,908 sites devoted to the Y2K problem—what techno-nerds call the year 2000 computer-glitch problem. I logged on to a chat line, and one person there seemed to believe that it was all the fault of Chris Carter, originator of *The X Files*.

Another person, calling himself, with massive originality, "The Phantom" claimed the CIA was behind it all and that all computers are being manipulated by Jimmy Hoffa and JFK from a hidden island in the Carribbean. I logged on with my real name.

:RINGER
>>I have a theory that I think far surpasses anything you people have been considering.

THE PHANTOM
>>Yeah? Identify location and security clearance.

:RINGER
>>Washington, and that's classified.

TOM TERRIFIC
>>The Y2K problem is intransigent, Ringer, an enigma wrapped in a nautilus. Best evidence is that it was engineered in a secret meeting in '93 between Bill Gates and the ambassador from the planet Zorf.

:RINGER
>>I can't go into my security rating or why I know what I know, but I know what I know, and that's all that I know.

THE PHANTOM
>>Okay. We're listening.

:RINGER
>>Have you ever seen Oliver Stone and a large parallel-processing computer in a room at the same time? Think about it. Oliver Stone made a movie about Jim Garrison and the murder of JFK. "Garrison" is also the name for a military installation, and the initials JFK also stand for Jeep Formation Killing—a rare World War II assassination strategy. "Jim" could also be construed as "gym" and "Stone" as rock. Can't you see? Can't you see? Do you need a freaking Rosetta Stone?

TOM TERRIFIC
>>Oh my gosh!

THE PHANTOM
>>Ringer, have you told this to anybody else? I am, like, a wad of chills.

:RINGER
>>More later. I hear footsteps. What? Not the claw!

Then I clicked off. Ain't I a stinker? Anyway, here, finally, is my test on the Y2K Problem for all you computer geniuses. Please do not look on your neighbor's paper or a meterorite will fall on your dog.

1. What would you call the microprocessor in Pat Robertson's computer?

>>A. The Repentium.

>>B. The 80666.

>>C. Jonah.

>>D. "Little Pat."

2. What do you think will happen to checking accounts as we come into the year 2000?

>>A. They will all suddenly balance to the penny.

>>B. All your money will be sent back to the year 1900 and made available to your great-grandmother, who will use it to buy canning equipment.

>>C. Every account will be automatically docked $12 to provide funds for

Lyle Lovett's hair surgery.

>>D. Nothing.

3. What effect will the Y2K problem likely have on the U.S. Postal Service?

>>A. Al Gore will seek funds for a
    satellite that will give every
    American a twenty-four-hour view of
    the post office in Nashville.

>>B. The P.O. will add a new category
    called Snail Mail that promises your
    letters will be delivered "whenever
    the hell we feel like it."

>>C. The Singing Telegram will return,
    with has-been singers doing the
    work. A Wayne Newton-gram will be
    eight dollars. George Michael will
    work for tips.

>>D. Your mail will be delivered by dogs
    trained to bite your pants legs.

4. What is the likely outcome of Y2K on scientific calculations?

>>A. Mathematicians will redefine *pi* as "around three or something."

>>B. Because of errors in calculation, the Space Shuttle, instead of going into an orbit 223 miles above the Earth, will go to Cleveland.

>>C. Statistical sampling for the U.S. Census will show that there are eight people in the United States, and all of them are dead.

>>D. Fermat's Last Theorem will be revealed as a code for "*Sacre bleu!* I forgot to get Beaujolais for the orgy!"

5. Who is most likely to benefit from this glitch and why?

>>A. Donny Osmond, and that's classified.

>>B. Roseanne. You gotta problem with that, pinhead?

>>C. Ellen DeGeneres. She plans to use money gathered during the Financial Panic to have her whine removed.

>>D. Richard Nixon. Thought he was dead, didn't you?

6. What will happen to your home computer when the year 2000 comes in?

>>A. It will crash.

>>B. It will levitate and float around the room and sing "Feelings."

>>C. It will start speaking to you and say, "Dave, you don't really want to do that do you? You don't really want to turn me off? Dave?"

>>D. It will send e-mail to your boss calling him "a loud-mouthed moron."

7. What will happen to Bill Gates and Microsoft during the height of the Y2K problem?

>>A. Bill will declare bankruptcy and issue a statement saying that Microsoft Explorer "was just a pale imitation of Netscape anyway."

>>B. Microsoft will announce they have

invented the MicroFilter, a computer
that makes cappuccino and serves a
toasted bagel every morning.

>>D. Gates will announce he's the presi-
dent of Mars and run away to Sri
Lanka with Pia Zadora.

>>E. Microsoft will invest $15 billion
in Viagra.

8. What business is likely to suffer the most because of the problem?

>>A. None of the above.

>>B. All of the above.

>>C. The above.

>>D. Not the above.

9. You are flying to Las Vegas with a head wind of ninety knots, but you are diverted to Chicago because of electrical problems. The problem corrects itself when you are sixty-three miles from O'Hare and you then fly on to Las Vegas but are slowed because of a five-degree shift in the jet stream. What will the in-flight meal taste like?

>>A. Cardboard.

>>B. A five-star gourmet feast.

>>C. That paste you used in kindergarten
that one kid was always licking off
the back of a drawing of his dog.

>>D. Better than botulism but worse than
salmonella.

10. What in the heck does question nine have to do with the Y2K problem?

>>A. Everything.

>>B. Nothing.

>>C. The plane had actually never left La
Guardia but computers said it had.

>>D. Your captain will explain it to you
later.

Yeow, the old Ringerman's worn himself out. I'm going to take a catnap.

Chapter Seventeen

As Lord Byron would say, things have gone from bad to verse.

Mollie got home from shopping last night, and Jerry had taken the kids to see the new animated movie from Don Bluth at the multiplex. Me, I can't take that much pastel in a sitting. So it was me and Mollie and Chico. Mollie was in a good mood because she'd been in Atlanta with her sister, but she was wary because I kept following her around.

First, I had to get rid of Chico, so I led him outside through the dog door. It was starry and moony. A dog down the street was having a barking fit.

"Chico, have you ever considered the universe?" I asked. I pointed my whiskers up. Chico looked up, squinting. It's a long way to heaven for a chihuahua.

"I want a soup bone," he said. This wasn't going to be easy.

"No, no, look up there into the stars," I said. He did. "Has it ever occurred to you that there is a whole planet that's nothing but a soup bone, and it's filled with happy dogs who eat the world all day?"

"Gaw," said Chico. "You think so?"

"I think it might come down if you called it," I said.

"Just called it?" he said. I was feeling like a stinker. I didn't mind.

"Bark for it, Chico, and the Planet Soup Bone might land in your backyard," I whispered. So the little needle-nose began to hrumpf and bark and finally start a series of semi-pathetic yowls and howls. I left him there and traipsed back through the dew-damp grass to the house. I like traipsing almost as much as I like sauntering.

Mollie was in the kitchen making a pitcher of frozen strawberry daiquiris. I jumped on the counter across from her and sat on my haunches and waited for her to speak.

"Ringer, I had a great day today shopping," she said. She was vamping, killing time. "And Jerry and the kids are out of the house, and I'm making something nice to drink, and then I'm going to watch *Gone With the Wind* on Turner Classic Movies. I'm feeling much better. I thought I was going crazy, you know?" She threw off a small, unconvincing giggle. "I mean, I thought I heard you speak. The human mind can play the strangest tricks."

She came over and rubbed me, and I arched up and sauntered around a little, careful not to knock over the salt and pepper.

"You want some Purina Cat Chow before the movie starts?" she asked.

"Actually, I'd like a daiquiri and some peanuts," I said. She backed across the room like like a crab and jumped seat-first up on the counter. Her eyes were huge. She looked into her hands.

"What is this?" she said.

"You could do Lady MacBeth's speech here, but it's not going to change things," I said mildly. "Mollie, come on, girl. You're my best friend. Look up at me and stop this cringing stuff."

She didn't look up at me. The daiquiris kept grinding away. Then, slowly, her face rose and she looked at me with narrowed eyes, and she let out a long breath.

"It's funny, but I thought I was crazy, and now I just think it's the world that's crazy," she said.

"Confucius said, 'Woman is the inheritor of wisdom if she can but shed her tendency toward putting things into small, pointless categories,'" I said.

"Confucius didn't say that."

"Okay, I made it up," I admitted. "But Mollie, animals *can* talk. We're not supposed to talk to humans, but I slipped up. Now, can we stop this *Exorcist* stuff? Besides, I never could remember the name of the guy who wrote that book. It was William Peter Blatty, but I always said 'William Petey Bladder.'"

Mollie barked out a choking laugh, her stomach shaking. Looooove that Mollie!

"But I *know* this is about the Millennium," she said. "I'm talking to a cat. Heavenly days. And Ringer, you're not just a cat. You have intelligence."

"Don't forget wit and sass," I said.

"I could book you on Letterman," she said. She still seemed in a fog. She turned off the daiquiris and poured herself a pink glass to the brim, took a sip, and licked her lips.

"I'll say nothing but *meow*, and Letterman will call you a stupid human," I said.

"So you're not going to talk to anybody but me?" she asked.

"I alone have escaped to speak to thee," I said.

"Literary, too."

"I've read everything you ever wrote," I said. "Masterpieces all."

"I don't believe it."

Then, after a pause, she said, "I've lost it. Gone around the bend. I'm talking to a cat, and he's talking back to me. Is it the Millennium? I read strange things might start to happen, but hearing a big, old, plain, gray cat talk?"

"Plain?" I said.

"And all the computers are going to go ballistic, and maybe UFOs will come down from outer space and reveal the secret of their world," she said.

"They're coming from the Planet Soup Bone," I muttered.

"And maybe there will be peace beyond the planets, and love beyond the stars."

"That's the Age of Aquarius, Mollie," I sighed. "At least get your clichés right." She took another long sip of her daiquiri.

"Maybe Ringer isn't real," she speculated. "Maybe there's never been a Ringer here at all, and my brain is just working too hard.

93

After all, I do write children's books. And darn good ones."

"Not according to *Kirkus*, at least for the last one," I said.

"*Kirkus*! Who . . . what do you know about book reviews?" she asked. "Wait, don't tell me. This is all in my mind."

"Michiko Kakutani of *The New York Times* is okay, but she's no Edmund Wilson," I said. "Or Alfred Kazin, for that matter."

"Hah," said Mollie. "My mind playing tricks on me. I bet if I ask you the name of my Uncle Al's business you could tell me that."

"Weird Al's Pre-Owned Imports," I said triumphantly. "You and Jerry have loaned him money to keep afloat for years, which I will never understand."

"Hah!" cried Mollie. "You *can't* be real! No stupid cat could possibly know about my Uncle Al!"

"Stupid?!" I bristled. "Want to see me do some calculus? Recite one of John Ashbery's longer poems?"

"But wait," she said. "If he's not real, why am I putting food out for him? I could save money."

"Whoa, let's not get too weird here, Molls," I said.

"Chico must be eating the extra food."

"Chico's in the backyard howling for the Planet Soup Bone!" I cried. "Mollie, look at me, I'm fur and blood!"

But it was no use. With that, she swept into the den and turned on TCM. Scarlett was already taunting the Tarleton Twins, but Mollie didn't seem to mind missing the credits. I didn't know what to do. At first, she thought I was a demon, and now she had convinced herself that I didn't exist at all. This Millennium stuff was starting to really hiss me off.

I let myself outside where Chico was still yelling at the sky and slipped past him down to Snowball's house. Desperate men will do anything. I found Snowball sitting alone in the middle of the warm grass of her backyard. She waved at me with her head when I came close. I curled up not far away. Once I'd come under similar circumstances and we wound up bathing each other. I'd always regretted that night.

"What's wrong, Ringer?" she asked. "Why so glum?"

"My friend Mollie thinks I don't exist anymore," I said. "She thinks I never existed at all."

"Well, that's not fair."

"You're darn tootin' it's not fair," I said. "It's awful. I don't know what to do next."

"You, Rinnnngeerrrrr?" she said. "I don't believe that." She was flirting with me. This was going to test my will power.

"It's true."

"If you aren't real, what are you?" she asked. "Are you a spook cat? My mama told me about spook cats, said they come out of the ground on Halloween and drag off bad little kittens."

"Child abuse," I muttered. "Why do adults tell those kinds of stories to kids?"

"Oh, it's true," she said. "Lots of evil things come up out of the ground, like possums and mushrooms and grass." I tried to think of a way to let it drop, to let Snowball's usual train of thought pass. I couldn't.

"What in the name of tarnation is evil about grass and mushrooms?" I asked.

"I get sick when I eat them," she said.

"Then don't eat them!" I cried. "Are you an idiot, Snowball?"

"Don't shout at me," she whined. "I get skin allergies when cats shout at me. I break out into these huge open sores and . . ."

"That's more than I need to know," I said. I thought I might hurl. "Sorry to bother you. I have to go home so Mollie can pretend I don't exist."

"Well, you don't have to be so snippy," she said.

I couldn't take any more of Snowball, and I was vaguely glad of it. Maybe it was better to go hide and lick my own wounds. Now I had lost Mollie, and I wasn't at all sure how I'd win her back. Chico had given up on calling the Planet Soup Bone and was gone, probably back inside to watch Rhett Butler with Mollie.

Maybe I was the victim of my own wit and sass. Maybe there was nothing for me to do but take The Big Wander. That's what cats do when they feel like they have lost their sense of place. We go on The Big Wander and wind up living in a double-wide with Wade and Lucille and eating scraps from a Dumpster. I could get run over by a rusted-out Chevelle while carrying a crusty Spam can across the highway.

I shuddered. I wasn't ready for The Big Wander. I needed something to distract me while I considered my plight. I knew what I'd do. Wait until Jerry and the kids got home and everybody was in bed, and then I'd come up with an essay test on the Millennium. It wouldn't solve anything, but at least I'd stay busy.

Idle paws are the devil's workshop.

Chapter Eighteen

It's midnight. Standard Cat Time. Annie and Buck got home with Jerry, and I watched the family from under the dining room table. Mollie didn't say much except that she was sick of Scarlett O'Hara's whining and would probably never watch *GWTW* again. Fat chance.

Annie came and found me.

"Ringer, what are you doing way back there under the table?" she asked. Trying to figure out how to save my career as the McGee "companion animal." (That's what veterinarians and some misguided people call us now. We're *pets*. That's all we want to be. We're not your companions. You're our companion *people*. Deal with it.) I backed up farther away. I didn't feel like company, and I sure didn't want to get dressed up as Raggedy Anne.

"What are you doing in there, Princess?" Jerry said. "It's late. You need to get to bed."

"Ringer's acting weird," said Annie. Mollie leaped out of her chair and came and took her daughter by the arm.

"He may have rabies or something," said Mollie. "Don't get near him."

"Rabies?" said Annie. "Is Ringer sick?" This wasn't a time for wit or sass. I came running out, trying my best to cough up a purr or two, walking on my toes, and bumping into Annie's legs.

"Well, maybe it's something else, scabies, I meant," said Mollie. At the mention of scabies, Jerry came stomping into the dining room for a look. Ack. The next thing you know, he'd be sticking needles in my flank to see what makes me sneeze. I fled. I went outside and lay in the dirt beneath a gardenia bush until they were all asleep.

Now, it's midnight, and here I am, Ringer the Bold, Ringer the Undefeated, typing on Mollie's computer. Here is your essay test on the Millennium. Pass or you have to spend another year in the twelfth grade.

1. **The missile system on an F-15 jet has not yet been cleared of the Y2K problem by the Department of Defense. When the plane fires its missiles in combat, are they more likely to hit their intended target or Pat Sajak? Why?**

2. The Internal Revenue Service is so far behind in its debugging efforts that it may have no ability to process tax returns in 2000. If you try to deduct a swimming pool as a medical expense, will you get sent to federal prison or on an all-expenses-paid trip to Cannes?

3. The Federal Aviation Administration has 630 critical systems that may quit in 2000, but which they promise will be fixed by 2004. If you are in a plane flying from New York to Los Angeles and 318 of the critical systems go down, will you arrive on time, late, or on the set of "Godzilla II?"

4. Estimates of the costs to fix the Y2K problem range as high as $600 billion. If you had $600 billion, would you invite Bill Gates to dinner or invent a Web browser and force him to use it every day for the rest of his life?

5. The rumor has spread wildly that all elevators will stop on January 1, 2000. The Otis Elevator Co. says it's an urban myth. If it were true, which New York building would you least like to be stuck in and why? And had you rather be stuck in an elevator with Bill Clinton or Pee-Wee Herman? Why?

6. If all the electrical power goes down because of the Y2K problem, will you be more likely to read "War and Peace" by candlelight or "Playboy" by a Coleman lantern?

7. Write an essay describing what you and Vanna White would discuss if you were both on an electric train that could never stop again because of the Millennium Problem. Essay must be at least nine words long.

8. What person would you most like to smack upside the head on January 1, 2000? Really? Why Bryant Gumbel?

This is fun, but I'm just vamping. I've got to face this Mollie problem head on and convince her that I can talk and it's not because of the Millennium. So I'm going to get a good night's sleep and see what happens tomorrow morning when the kids are at school and Jerry's gone to his office. Mollie does her writing and then gardens.

I'm going to wait until she's happily digging in the ground and see if we can have this out.

Chapter Nineteen

I awoke when Mollie was packing the family off for the day, and then I went and chewed the fat with John the Beagle for a while. I don't know where he got the fat, but it was really good. I wanted to confide in John, but I wasn't sure he'd keep my secret. Dogs are the world's worst gossips.

"Why the long face, Ringer?" asked John. "I've given you half the fat here, and you're lapping it up like Drew Carey."

"John, can I confide in you?" I said. He nodded. I washed my face. My sentences got short. I felt like I was in a Mickey Spillane novel.

"Sure," he said.

"I have a friend who is in some trouble, and I don't know how to help him out," I said. "He did a stupid thing, and now he's terrified that he's going to be caught."

"What did this friend do?" asked John.

"He spoke to his humans," I said. John nodded amiably.

"Oh, that's easy," he said. "We will bite his tail off and chase him into the sewers. Oooooo. Just like *Les Miserables*." Then he laughed and kept chewing his hunk of meat.

"Uh huh," I said. "Well, I'll pass that on." Maybe John knew it was me, but he was too good a friend to bring it back up. Just then, Fluffy, the new black cat, ambled up. I've never liked ambling as much as sauntering, but it does make a fashion statement.

"Hi, boys," she said. "I see you're just chewing the fat."

"You can have mine," I said. "I'm leaving. I've got to go home."

"Do you know what Simone de Beauvoir said about living from the fat of the land?" asked Fluffy. I was starting to miss Snowball.

"No, I don't," I said. "And I don't want to know, thanks." I turned to leave. "Did she say anything about the Millennium?"

"Beats me," said Fluffy. "I read this fat thing in *Reader's Digest*." Maybe Fluffy wasn't so bad after all.

It was time to confront Mollie once and for all. We needed to have this out, because the worry was wrecking my sleep, and I was losing interest in being a Thinking Cat. I walked slowly back through the sunny yards and listened to the insects singing and speaking. Birds went through their arias, except for a crow who sounded like a car backing over a whoopee cushion.

Mollie was on her knees in the backyard planting some marigolds. They stink but make pretty flowers, and so I stood aside for a moment and let her finish then sit back up. She looked at me darkly. I wasn't sure what she was going to say.

"But if there really is a Ringer, and he's not talking, then maybe I've gone around the bend," she said. "I'll wind up doing macramé and watching *The Rosie O'Donnell Show*."

I couldn't let this go on. Ringer the Bold had to intervene. I spoke softly and slowly.

"Mollie, I can talk and this *is* real," I said. She didn't flinch or run. "And I'm your buddy, remember? And it's not because of the Millennium. You human people don't know everything about the world. And it upsets you to find out you don't. You're going to have to talk to me some time."

"But even if you are real, and even if I'm not bonkers, how could you know so much?" she said.

"I live here!" I said. "I read books. I watch television. I use the Internet. In fact, I'm writing a book right now." She started laughing. A bee came down and sniffed around the marigolds and yelled "Pee-you!" and buzzed off. Bees are impatient creatures.

"I can see you right here and now," she said mildly. "And I don't feel crazy. And yet I must be crazy because I'm talking to a cat, and he's talking back to me. I don't know what else it could be."

"Ask me anything about you, Mollie," I said. "Anything at all. I'll prove to you that I know all about you. This ain't animatronics, you know."

"Okay, wise cat, what's my favorite color?" she blurted.

"Yellow."

"What was the name of my first book?"

"*A Garden for the Children*," I said. "It was a finalist for the Newberry Award. I always thought you got cheated." She laughed. I walked over and sat right next to her.

"What happened to me on a trip to Maine two years ago?"

"You were in a wreck and broke your left arm," I said. "I lay on it for a week after you got back, remember? And the doctor told you it healed faster than any break he'd ever seen. I *purred* it better."

She began to rub me down the length of my back. Yum. Love that Mollie!

"What's the most important thing in the world to me?" she asked.

"The same as it is for me," I said. "Our family. Once you were drinking some coffee in the kitchen, and you stopped to look at a family picture stuck on the fridge with magnets and do you know what you said? You said, 'Lord, how I love them.' Yes, you did."

"I did. I remember that. You were there?"

"I was inside the pantry playing with a twist-tie. And you took that picture off the fridge, and you kissed your husband and kids on the face, each one of them in order. Mollie, I never saw a thing in my life that touched me so much. That's how much *I* love *you*."

"You must be real," she said. "Nobody can imagine a love that strong."

"Do you know what Simone de Beauvoir said about love?" I asked.

"No."

"Well, neither do I, but anyway."

She laughed and kept rubbing my back. I stretched and looked around. A tiger swallowtail was flitting around. They can't speak so they spread their message in dance. She was happy, no doubt about it. The Bolshoi Ballet would be lucky to have a tiger swallowtail.

"I guess it's not about the Millennium, then?"

"It's about friends," I said. "You're my friend, and you always will be." Her face shone from an inner light. She let out a long sigh.

"Okay then," she said. "I'll just have to accept the fact that you are you and I am me and we can talk."

"Gee, this is turning into something for the self-help section," I said. "Next thing you know, you'll be telling me the problems of two people don't amount to a hill of beans in this crazy world."

"They do," she said. Her smile was dazzling. "The world is only about the problems and love of two people. Just two at a time. If it's done right."

"You do it right, kiddo," I said, trying not to get maudlin. "You do it right."

We spent the rest of the day together, and I didn't say too much. I helped her do the Sunday crossword puzzle from *The New York Times*, which she'd been saving. I think I knew more words than she did, but I shouldn't boast. We finished it in forty-five minutes.

I slept on her feet as usual that night.

"Sweet dreams, Ringer," she said. Jerry was already snoring. I winked at her and rolled into my dreams.

Chapter Twenty

Freed from the burden of my friend's worry, I clawed my way back into the Millennium problem with gusto. It was time for Ringer to make some predictions about what will happen in the Millennium. I showed Mollie what I had done so far, and she said she'd talk to her friend who's an editor at Hill Street Press about publishing it. Me and Mollie, published authors!

So here's another multiple choice quiz about what personalities will blossom after the turn of the New Millennium and why.

1. **Which of the following is most likely to become the first president elected after the turn of the century and why?**

>>A. Jerry Falwell, because God is on his side.

>>B. Dick Gephardt, because God thinks Jerry Falwell is a small-minded, self-centered little rat.

>>C. John F. Kennedy Jr., because of his native charisma, his family's fund-raising ability, and his endorsement from *George* magazine.

>>D. Charleton Heston, because he will shoot you if you don't vote for him.

2. **Who will be the next superstar in the movies?**

>>A. Don Knotts will make a comeback, playing Moses in a new version of *The Ten Commandments*.

>>B. "Steve Erkel" who will realize he is never going to achieve puberty and will star in a series of new "Andy Hardy" movies.

107

>>C. Pia Zadora will have a breakout performance playing Spartacus as sword-and-sandal remakes become popular.

>>D. Sam Donaldson, who will co-star with Julie Christie in a sequel to *Dr. Zhivago* called *Lara and the Arrogant, Egotistical News Flak*.

3. What author will become the best-seller in the New Millennium?

>>A. Charles Frazier, author of *Cold Mountain*, because of his huge talent.

>>B. James Frazer, author of *The Golden Bough*, who will make a comeback after being dead since 1941.

>>C. Frasier, from the sitcom, because people like the show and really don't have any taste in reading.

>>D. Frozier, a dog in Kansas who writes gooey books about his grandmother.

4. Who will win the software/computer wars and why?

>>A. Microsoft because Bill Gates will foreclose on your mortgage if you don't buy from him.

>>B. Intel, with their new microprocessor called The Big Kahuna, which is so fast and smart it can program your VCR.

>>C. Microhard, a spin-off by disgruntled former employees of Bill Gates because they will develop software that allows you to deduct pay from congressmembers who are loud-mouthed morons.

>>D. Outtel, a spin-off by disgruntled former employees of Intel, with their new chip that digitizes mothers-in-law.

5. Who will the greatest singing star be after the turn of the century?

>>A. Courtney Love. If you don't buy her records, she'll come to your house and shriek.

>>B. LeAnn Rimes, who will change over from country to opera and become a sensation as a Rhine maiden.

>>C. Tony Bennett, who will still be working clubs well into his 120s.

>>D. All rappers, who will wake up on January 1, 2000, and say, "Wait a minute—there's no music to this stuff."

Whew, this studying of the Millennium has been nothing but hard work. I trust that you have been attentive and that you have not cheated on all my tests!

After I got through writing this morning, I went back outside and wandered around until I saw Buster, Larry, and Snowball sitting in the low limbs of a magnolia tree in the Nicholson's yard. They were chatting amiably.

"Hey, Ringeerrrr," said Snowball. "You won't believe what Buster did this morning, just won't believe it." I climbed up beside them on a limb and tucked up. Climbing's fun, but nothing like sauntering. Buster looked like the cat who ate the canary.

"Ate a canary?" I asked.

"A whippoorwill!" cried Snowball. "He brought it over, and he and I shared it for breakfast!"

"Now look what you've done," I said. "A poor, defenseless bird, flapping about pleasantly in the spring air, and you pounce on it, Buster, and kill it and then eat it? It probably has family and friends still waiting on it back at the nest. You should be ashamed." They all looked at me as if I'd gone around the bend. Larry walked over and banged me on the head a couple of times with his paw.

"Earth to Ringer," he said. "Earth to Ringer! I hate to break the news to you, big guy, but cats eat birds. Cats eat mice. Dogs eat cats. If we had lions, they'd eat dogs. We're smack dab in the middle of the food chain. Have you joined the Democratic Party or something?"

"Maybe with the New Millennium, it will be the dawning of the Age of Aquarius," I said. "Harmony and understanding, sympathy and trust will abound." They looked at each other.

"Naaahhhhh," they all said.

"You're really hung up on this Millennium stuff, aren't you?" said Larry. "I thought you of all people wouldn't be out there in left field with the tree huggers and crystal lickers."

"Maybe I just understand a little better why you have to live life slowly and not judge people too harshly," I said. "Maybe they're just doing the best they can to get by." They all looked at me in silence for a moment.

"I could hire a bulldog to kick him around a little bit," said Buster. "Not kill him, just grab him by the neck and waggle him until his senses come back."

"I'm surprised at all of you," I said. "I'm just saying maybe I've grown a little bit while I was thinking about what's going to happen at the turn of the century."

"But what about meeeeee?" said Snowball. She arched up and started walking around all of us. Larry held his place and so did I, but Buster couldn't help himself. He tried to grab her when she swung past, and he fell off his limb and was hanging on only by his claws.

"Hey, you guys!" he said. Then he slipped and fell off. But we were only about four feet up, so he landed softly. "Well, thanks boatloads for all the help."

"You boys are so cruel," said Snowball. She jumped down and arched around, brushing up against Buster. He looked up at me and Larry and shrugged. Being an animal means being an animal. We both understood. They went off whispering.

I stretched and sighed. It felt good to be alive.

"So what happened about you talking to your friend?" whispered Larry.

"I think it all worked out," I said.

"Wait, I can seeeeeee it now," said Larry. He put his paw to his forehead and acted as if he were having a vision. "He looked into his crystal and saw that Taurus was entering Uranus."

"Very funny, smart guy," I said. "But I happen to know it was a serious problem. And how come you didn't come tell me about the whippoorwill? Huh? I thought we were buddies? All for one and one for all? I thought nothing was ever going to come between us?"

There was a rustling below us, and we both turned in time to see Fluffy sashaying across the grass. Girls can sashay but boys can't. On the other hand, girls are awful at sauntering. It's just the way things are.

"Well, it's boys' morning out," said Fluffy. We both jumped out of the tree and landed at her feet and then looked at each other and grinned. Some things are hardwired, no doubt about it.

"I was just rereading Proust this morning," I said. "Let me ask you—which do you like better, *Swann's Way* or *Cities of the Plain*?"

"Actually, I never could read Proust," she said. "I've *slept* on Proust, though. I think most people sleep on Proust." I laughed.

"You're probably right."

"I haven't read Proust and don't intend to," said Larry. "I'm just a plain cat. Maybe a Louis L'Amour or a Robert Parker "Spenser" mystery once in a while, but no Proust."

"Ohhhhh, I love Spenser!" cried Fluffy. "Don't you just adore how Spenser loves Susan Silverman? How romantic!"

"I thought you were a slightly cynical riot-grrrl," I said. She looked at me like women look at men.

"Come on, let's go through some of the plots," said Larry. "Did you read *Looking for Rachel Wallace*?"

And just like that, they were gone through a broken slat in the fence, heads close together. Well, I'd missed out on the whippoor-will, Snowball had gone off with Buster, and Larry had snatched Fluffy right from under my whiskers. But I didn't mind very much.

Life goes on. The Ringerman has only just begun to think.

Chapter Twenty-One

So that's how Mollie and I became even better friends. Every day, she sends the kids off to school and Jerry to his office so he can stick needles in people and make them sneeze. Annie still dresses me up as Raggedy Anne, and Buck still sets things on fire from time to time. Just a regular family.

After everybody's gone, Mollie makes cappuccino. One morning, she poured some cappuccino in a bowl for me and asked me how I liked it. I lapped a bit up.

"Tastes like mud-puddle water," I said.

"Sorry, Ringer," she said.

"Sorry?" I said. "I *love* mud-puddle water. I used to think it was kind of gross, but then my friend John the Beagle told me something that I've always remembered."

"What?" asked Mollie. She was making us a bagel with cream cheese. Yum.

"Remember that when you look closely enough in a mud puddle, the only thing you see is *you*," I said.

"Aw, that's sweet," said Mollie.

"I thought it was kind of feeble," I said. "Never take advice from a dog. They mean well, but the cat's where it's at."

"Incidentally, Ringer, I was looking over what you've been writing on my computer, and what's this stuff about Pierre du Pint and Sartre de Jaré Lewis?" she asked. "Were those real people?"

I shrugged and came over and lapped up some of the cream cheese from my bagel. Tart but not tangy—a sensation for the palate.

"Actually, anything is true if you believe it long and hard enough," I said. Mollie stared at me as she sipped her cappuccino.

"That's the most ridiculous thing I've ever heard," she said.

"Well, sue me, I'm addicted to homilies," I said. "People will believe anything if they think about it long enough. Me, I'm just looking for a loaf of bread, a jug of wine, and thou."

Mollie laughed that laugh. I gnawed on my bagel for while and then stretched.

"I think I'll go outside for a while and take a nap while you write," I said. "Who knows, me and my friend Larry might go vole hunting this afternoon."

"You actually eat those things?" she said.

"Nah, but they sing like nobody's business," I said.

Mollie rubbed me on her way toward the computer. I went outside past the sleeping Chico, whose stomach was making hideous noises. I walked into the deep grass and stretched and sat down and thought about things. Maybe being a writer *was* a pretty good life for a cat. Maybe I should spend all of my time inside at the computer instead of out here. Maybe my time catting around was over.

"Hi there, big boy," said a voice from the bushes. I turned to see Fluffy come walking out, tail up waving at me.

"Fluffy, I thought you went off with Larry," I said. "Run out of Spenser plots to deconstruct?"

"Larry's great," she said. She came over near me and sat down. She had bathed, and her fur shone in the sunlight. "But he doesn't really have a sense of humor. I like a sense of humor in a guy."

"I thought I had humor once, but it turned out to be just a hairball," I said. She giggled. Oh my. I started to saunter across the yard, and Fluffy came after me. Just as we got to the edge of the yard, I glanced back over my shoulder and saw Mollie looking at us out the window of her study.

In the morning light, her smiling eyes were as clear as crystal.